Accountability and Oversight of US Exchange Rate Policy

Accountability and Oversight of US Exchange Rate Policy

C. RANDALL HENNING

Peterson Institute for International Economics
Washington, DC
June 2008

C. Randall Henning, visiting fellow, has been associated with the Institute since 1986. He serves on the faculty of the School of International Service, American University. He specializes in the politics and institutions of international economic relations, international and comparative political economy, and regional integration. His research work focuses on international monetary policy, European monetary integration, macroeconomic policy coordination, finance G-7 and G-8 summit cooperation, and regional cooperation in East Asia. He is the author of *East Asian Financial Cooperation* (2002), *The Exchange Stabilization Fund: Slush Money or War Chest?* (1999), *Cooperating with Europe's Monetary Union* (1997), *Currencies and Politics in the United States, Germany, and Japan* (1994), and recent journal articles on exchange rate policymaking in the euro area; coauthor of *Transatlantic Perspectives on the Euro* (2000), *Global Economic Leadership and the Group of Seven* (1996) with C. Fred Bergsten, *Can Nations Agree? Issues in International Economic Cooperation* (1989), and *Dollar Politics: Exchange Rate Policymaking in the United States* (1989); and coeditor of *Governing the World's Money* (2002). He has testified to several congressional committees and served as the European Community Studies Association Distinguished Scholar and as Faculty President of the School of International Service at American University.

**PETER G. PETERSON INSTITUTE
FOR INTERNATIONAL ECONOMICS**
1750 Massachusetts Avenue, NW
Washington, DC 20036-1903
(202) 328-9000   FAX: (202) 659-3225
www.petersoninstitute.org

C. Fred Bergsten, *Director*
Edward Tureen, *Director of Publications,
  Marketing, and Web Development*

*Typesetting by Xcel Graphic Services
Printing by Kirby Lithographic Company, Inc.
Cover by Jody Billert/Design Literate, Inc.*

Printed in the United States of America
10 09 08   5 4 3 2 1

Library of Congress Cataloging-in-Publication Data

Henning, C. Randall.
  Accountability and oversight of US exchange rate policy / C. Randall Henning.
     p. cm.
  ISBN-13: 978-0-88132-419-8 (alk. paper)
  1. Foreign exchange rates—United States. 2. United States—Foreign economic relations. 3. Monetary policy—United States. 4. Legislative oversight—United States. I. Title.

HG3909.H458 2008
332.4'560973—dc22
                              2008019390

HG
3903
H458
2008

To Nathaniel and Nick,
who apply rigorous oversight and
exacting standards of accountability

Contents

Figures

Several other Institute publications are also inspired by the current global balance-of-payments adjustment problem. The Institute has recently published an in-depth examination of the debate over Chinese exchange rate policy, *Debating China's Exchange Rate Policy* (2008) edited by Morris Goldstein and Nicholas Lardy, *Reference Rates and the International Monetary System* (2007) by John Williamson, *US-China Trade Disputes: Rising Tide, Rising Stakes* (2006) by Gary C. Hufbauer, Yee Wong, and Ketki Sheth, and *The United States as a Debtor Nation* (2005) by William R. Cline. *Accountability and Oversight of US Exchange Rate Policy* complements these other studies.

The Peter G. Peterson Institute for International Economics is a private, nonprofit institution for the study and discussion of international economic policy. Its purpose is to analyze important issues in that area and to develop and communicate practical new approaches for dealing with them. The Institute is completely nonpartisan.

The Institute is funded by a highly diversified group of philanthropic foundations, private corporations, and interested individuals. About 30 percent of the Institute's resources in our latest fiscal year were provided by contributors outside the United States, including about 12 percent from Japan.

The Institute's Board of Directors bears overall responsibilities for the Institute and gives general guidance and approval to its research program, including the identification of topics that are likely to become important over the medium run (one to three years) and that should be addressed by the Institute. The director, working closely with the staff and outside Advisory Committee, is responsible for the development of particular projects and makes the final decision to publish an individual study.

The Institute hopes that its studies and other activities will contribute to building a stronger foundation for international economic policy around the world. We invite readers of these publications to let us know how they think we can best accomplish this objective.

C. FRED BERGSTEN
Director
May 2008

Acknowledgments

I wish to acknowledge the abundant advice, guidance, and support from several groups of people. First, I want to thank those people in congressional offices, executive agencies, and international organizations who agreed to interviews on a background basis over the course of this project. My meetings with them have been the most rewarding aspect of this research, and their input, judgments, and feedback have been critical to the study. Second, I wish to acknowledge C. Fred Bergsten for his enthusiasm for this subject and his encouragement, ideas, and feedback on the project. Third, I would like to recognize very helpful written comments on the manuscript from C. Fred Bergsten, Benjamin J. Cohen, I. M. Destler, Thomas Dorsey, Robert Fauver, Gary Clyde Hufbauer, Steven B. Kamin, Peter B. Kenen, Ellen Meade, David Mulford, Patrick A. Mulloy, Michael Mussa, Edwin M. Truman, Tessa van der Willigen, and John Williamson—with apologies to anyone who I might have inadvertently omitted. Fourth, I am also grateful for oral comments offered at several study group meetings, including one hosted by the Peterson Institute, from Bas B. Bakker, Robert Blecker, Julie Chon, Joseph E. Gagnon, Morris Goldstein, Martin J. Gruenberg, Kent Hughes, Jason Kearns, Albert Keidel, Sydney Key, Janis Lazda, Ross B. Leckow, James Lister, Scott Morris, Adam Posen, Ernest Preeg, Lex Rieffel, Howard Rosen, David Ross, Robert Solomon, Arvind Subramanian, Daniel K. Tarullo, and Franklin Vargo. The usual disclaimer applies: None of these people are responsible for any error or omission that might remain in the final manuscript. Fifth, I wish to acknowledge the indispensable and excellent research assistance of Marko Klasnja, who helped me throughout this project and prepared the charts and tables among numerous other contributions to this book. The study has greatly benefited from his sustained and thorough efforts. Finally, I wish to acknowledge the publications staff of the Peterson Institute—Marla Banov, Madona Devasahayam, and Ed Tureen, in particular—for once again competently shepherding my manuscript to publication.

C. RANDALL HENNING

1

Introduction

Exchange rate policy has become a particularly important issue for the US Congress in recent years. The issue's return to political prominence, a periodic feature of US international economic policies, has in this instance been driven largely by objections to China's exchange rate policy. Competition from China has placed economic pressure on US producers, who have complained to members of Congress that the Chinese currency, the renminbi, is substantially undervalued. Meanwhile, the US Treasury Department has refused to cite China in its semiannual reports to Congress as a country that "manipulates" its currency, despite unprecedented amounts of foreign exchange intervention by Chinese authorities to restrain their currency's appreciation. The Secretary of the Treasury, Henry M. Paulson, Jr. prefers a diplomatic approach to China in the form of the Strategic Economic Dialogue. Frustrated by what they perceive to be the modest results of these discussions, several members of Congress have proposed legislation that, if adopted, would reform the process by which Treasury identifies and responds to currency manipulation and could impose trade restrictions to compensate for undervaluation. The stakes are raised by the applicability of such provisions to countries beyond China whose economic strategies have also included substantial undervaluation of their currencies.

The relationship between Congress and the executive, in particular the Treasury Department, lies at the heart of the US response to China's economic policies and the broader challenge of international adjustment. The Exchange Rates and International Economic Policy Coordination Act of 1988, an important component of the large omnibus trade act that year, partly defined this relationship with respect to exchange rates. The Act mandated Treasury to report to Congress and the secretary to testify at follow-up hearings if asked to do so by the banking committees of the House and Senate. Proponents intended the Act to improve congressional oversight and Treasury's accountability on exchange rate policy. Congress thus involved itself in exchange rate policy more deeply than it had prior to the 1980s, and more deeply than the legislatures of most, if not all, of the other key currency countries.

Accountability in US exchange rate policy is important for two reasons. First, it is important to keep policies connected to the democratic process, both to sustain broad political support for those policies and to redirect them when they deviate in the extreme from broadly held preferences. Congressional oversight and legislation on exchange rate policy helped achieve both of these aims during the mid-1980s (Destler and Henning 1989). Second, the general and specific provisions of the 1988 Act bear heavily on the effective functioning and legitimate governance of the international economic system as a whole. In particular, they target currency practices that, if allowed to continue, would impede balance of payments adjustment and erode popular faith in the fairness of international trade and finance. In doing so, these provisions reinforce the rules and norms of the international monetary regime as reflected in the Articles of Agreement of the International Monetary Fund (IMF).

Three changes in the fundamental features of the US and global economies since the mid-1980s reinforce the importance of accountability and oversight in this policy area. First, the US economy is considerably more open to international trade than it was in the mid-1980s and far more open than at the outset of the postwar period. Exports plus imports relative to GDP was 9.3 percent in 1950, 18.4 percent in 1987, and 26.7 percent in 2005.[1] With a general increase in capital mobility, the US economy is also more open to international capital flows than in the early decades of the postwar period. Greater openness increases the magnitude of the macroeconomic and distributive effects of changes in the external value of the dollar. Second, with the rise of numerous emerging markets and more in the queue, the number and diversity of countries whose policies bear on US economic performance have risen apace. Third, within US politics, the partisanship of international economic policy has intensified, and splits in party control of the Congress and the executive create friction between the branches (see, for example, Destler 2005).

In light of these fundamental changes, and more immediately the disputes over Treasury's approach in its reports and numerous legislative proposals to change oversight, the time is ripe for an assessment of the Exchange Rates and International Economic Policy Coordination Act of 1988—hereafter referred to as the 1988 Act—and the reporting process

---

1. US Bureau of Economic Analysis data as reported in the 2007 *Economic Report of the President*, tables B-24, B-25, and B-103.

that they created. How have the provisions and the reporting process met key tests of accountability in practice? Has Treasury provided transparency sufficient for Congress to judge whether the department has met the objectives of this and other relevant legislation? Has Congress provided appropriate oversight? Has the process contributed to better policy and, if not, what reforms would be likely to improve policy outcomes? This book addresses these questions.

Premises

Before proceeding, it would be worth making the key premises of the analysis explicit. These relate to the location of authority over exchange rate policy, Chinese currency practices, the role of the IMF, and the scope for treating the exchange rate as a policy instrument.

First, this analysis proceeds from the fundamental assumption that the US Congress is the ultimate source of authority in exchange rate policy. Congress has delegated authority on this issue to the Treasury, and the Federal Reserve, and properly reserves the right to establish objectives for policy and exercise oversight. While these agencies exercise their mandate with considerable discretion, they are and should be answerable to Congress. This premise is developed further in the following section.

Second, Chinese foreign exchange intervention over 2002–07 was unprecedented in magnitude and contributed to growth in China's current account surplus to roughly 12 percent of GDP by 2007. Chinese policy is far outside the range of experience since the Second World War for systemically important countries. The analysis in this book rests on a basic judgment that this behavior harms the multilateral system and threatens its political underpinnings. Specifically, Chinese authorities' intervention has kept the renminbi substantially undervalued, prevented a desirable adjustment of current account imbalances, and constitutes "manipulation" as that term was meant to be interpreted by Congress.[2] It is important to point out that this is not an issue on which the respective countries' national economic interests, defined comprehensively, collide. To the contrary, by diverting resources to less productive uses, renminbi undervaluation both distorts Chinese development and harms growth elsewhere. Thus, China, the United States, and the rest of the

---

2. Goldstein (2006), Goldstein and Lardy (2005, 2008), and Mussa (2007) present compelling arguments that Chinese policy behavior violates the injunction against manipulation in the IMF's Articles of Agreement. See also C. Fred Bergsten, Statement before the Hearing on US Economic Relations with China: Strategies and Options on Exchange Rates and Market Access, Subcommittee on Security and International Trade and Finance, Committee on Banking, Housing and Urban Affairs, United States Senate, May 23, 2007. Similarly, the chapters that follow argue that Chinese behavior also contravenes the injunction against manipulation within the meaning of the 1988 Act.

world would all be better off with substantial further appreciation of the renminbi (Goldstein and Lardy 2005, 2008). In order to reduce the US current account deficit on a more lasting basis, a substantial further reduction in the US federal budget deficit is also desirable over the medium term; but the persistence of US fiscal deficits does not diminish the desirability of renminbi appreciation.

Third, the IMF is the best venue for addressing currency alignment, exchange rate policy, and payments adjustment. Among international institutions, the IMF has the comparative advantage, and it is the preferable forum for challenging countries' exchange rate policies within a multilateral context. However, the Fund's governing bodies are sometimes manifestly unwilling to confront members on such practices and, even if willing to do so, probably lack compelling means of enforcement. The governance and resources of the IMF are not always sufficient to combat currency practices that threaten or harm the international monetary system. The United States and other countries should therefore retain the means and reserve the right to discourage exchange rate policies of other IMF member states that impede adjustment, threaten stability, or contravene their obligations in the Fund.

Fourth, analysis of relations between Congress and the Treasury in this area rests on the prior finding that "exchange rate policy" is a meaningful concept. Some economists argue that the exchange rate is not a policy instrument that can be separated from other macroeconomic tools, mainly monetary and fiscal policy. The premise of this book is that, although the exchange rate depends largely on foreign and domestic macroeconomic policies, having a policy toward the external value of the currency is justified, and even necessary under certain circumstances.

Those adopting the "rational expectations" view of foreign exchange markets believe that participants act on complete information about macroeconomic policy, underlying economic conditions and the relationship between them. If this were accurate, there would be little or no scope for movement of the exchange rate from the level dictated by the fundamentals, no speculative bubbles in exchange markets, and no room for effective foreign exchange intervention. However, experience demonstrates that currencies frequently become unhinged from the fundamentals and exhibit substantial and prolonged misalignments. Market participants do not have access to complete information by any means and this creates scope for intervention of various sorts to be effective (Williamson 1998, 2007; de Grauwe and Grimaldi 2006). Consider, in turn, (1) the evolution of the professional consensus on the effectiveness of government action in the foreign exchange market and (2) the desirability of sometimes adjusting macroeconomic policies to manage the exchange rate and balance of payments.

Evaluation of the scope of government capacity to affect exchange rates without altering underlying monetary, fiscal, or structural policies is hobbled by the weakness of economists' models of exchange rate determination, which deprives analysts of reliable counterfactuals against which to measure the effects of government action in foreign exchange markets. The professional consensus on the effectiveness of intervention, as a consequence, has swung back and forth over the decades. The availability of daily intervention data over the last 10 years has improved these studies. More recent studies have also addressed more sophisticated questions, differentiating the circumstances under which intervention is and is not likely to be effective. As a result of this evolution, these more recent studies generally find intervention to be more effective than did studies conducted during the 1980s.[3] Experience with massive Chinese and Japanese interventions during the last five years suggests they can indeed be effective, even when sterilized, with and without capital controls, for extended periods.

The conditions that create scope for intervention to be at least partially effective also create scope for other more subtle instruments. In the presence of high capital mobility, flexible exchange rates are often driven by herd behavior and expectations, and are thus frequently disconnected from the underlying economic fundamentals. In addition, the foreign exchange markets often exhibit multiple equilibria. When private expectations are easily swayed, governments are more likely to be able to induce a shift from one equilibrium to another. Particularly when the rate moves far from equilibrium, governments might well coordinate the expectations of private participants by articulating an emerging consensus on the direction of movement (Taylor 2003).

Government officials can influence these expectations, depending on market sentiment, by signaling their desire for a stronger, weaker, or stable currency, by forswearing intervention, and by intervening. Under some market conditions, such as a profound current account imbalance, a "no comment" in the face of a significant exchange rate movement can be interpreted by the market as a clear signal of approval. Conflict over trade policy and market access can enhance the markets' sensitivity to official statements. Thus, even if US policymakers have only partial influence over the exchange rate, that influence can be substantial at particular junctures.

The debate among economists has moved a long way from asking simply whether intervention is effective, as was the tendency in the 1980s. Careful studies now ask under what circumstances intervention can be effective. Few if any would assert that particular settings of monetary and fiscal policy determine a unique exchange rate, or even a narrow range for the exchange rate, that is consistent with internal and external equilibrium. Further discussion is beyond the scope of this book, but suffice it to say that the balance of evidence suggests that government action can be successful under a variety of circumstances, such as when it is publicly

---

3. For a review, see Sarno and Taylor (2001).

announced, conducted jointly by two or more central banks, consistent with the underlying fundamentals, and taken when the exchange rate is far from equilibrium.[4]

Irrespective of the exogeneity of the exchange rate, moreover, there are instances when monetary and fiscal policy should be adjusted with the exchange rate and external balance in mind. A large economy such as the United States will usually set monetary and fiscal policy primarily with a view toward managing domestic output, employment, and inflation. Normally, the external balance and value of the currency will enter into these calculations primarily through their forecast impact on these domestic variables. However, when large current account deficits become unsustainable and the buildup of external debt inappropriate, there might be a strong case for adjusting macroeconomic policy to manage the external risks, in which case the exchange rate will be a crucial intermediate variable.

As this discussion suggests, the term "exchange rate policy" takes on an expansive meaning in this book. Exchange rate policy has multiple components: official declarations, foreign exchange intervention, and adjustments of other policies with exchange rate or external balance objectives in mind. The term includes official adoption of a view as to an appropriate value for the dollar, either on an effective basis or against a particular currency, and representation to that effect in international fora or bilateral meetings. The term also includes instances where the timing of adjustments of macroeconomic policies is advanced or delayed to affect the external value of the currency.

Comparative Perspective

Because this book assesses the accountability mechanism and identifies weaknesses on the way to proposing remedies, some of the relative strengths of US institutional arrangements should also be acknowledged at the outset. These strengths are more apparent in comparative perspective. This section first provides an international comparison and then a domestic comparison with accountability in other policy areas.

International

The US model, characterized by the relatively strong role for the Congress, compares favorably with the arrangements within the euro area as far as

---

4. See Catte, Galli, and Rebecchini (1994); Dominguez and Frankel (1993); Williamson (2000); Sarno and Taylor (2001); Ito (2002); Ramaswamy and Samiei (2003); Taylor (2003); Kubelec (2004); Fratzscher (2004); and de Grauwe and Grimaldi (2006). Genberg and Swoboda (2005) find official declarations to be significantly effective.

accountability and democratic control are concerned (Henning 2007a; see also Henning 2006). Indeed, the European Parliament's standing as the institution to hold the monetary authorities to account is weak, the relationship between the European Central Bank and the national finance ministers who constitute the Eurogroup is often contentious on exchange rate policy, and these institutions are not subject to oversight that is backed by a capacity to impose sanctions if standards have not been met or by any reporting requirement equivalent to the 1988 Act. When policy deviates from the preferences of a broad coalition of interest groups in the United States, as it did in the mid-1980s, Congress can threaten legislation on trade and exchange rates with credibility. No similar mechanism exists in the euro area. Institutional arrangements and accountability mechanisms, of which the exchange rate report is one example, give the legislature greater standing vis-à-vis core policymakers in the United States than in the euro area.

When compared against best practices in accountability mechanisms, however, exchange rate policy arrangements in the United States must be judged less favorably. Because US arrangements lie between best practices, on the one hand, and euro area arrangements, on the other, the comparison differs depending on the point of reference. It is quite consistent, therefore, to find that the US Treasury is more accountable than euro area monetary authorities, but that it has sometimes not lived up to the spirit of the 1988 Act. Although Congress plays a stronger role in the United States than any "outside" institution in the euro area, the US accountability process can certainly be improved.

Domestic

Exchange rate policy accountability can also be compared with executive branch reporting and congressional oversight in other policy areas. Treasury's exchange rate report is one of more than a hundred reports from the department mandated by Congress; these are in turn a fraction of the several thousand required of the executive branch as a whole.[5] Such reports have been a standard tool of congressional oversight and influence over policy administration since the 1930s. Treasury and other agencies report on foreign investment, trade policy and negotiations, and monetary policy, to name areas related to exchange rates, plus a number of foreign policy matters such as intelligence. Thus, rather than unusual, Treasury's reporting requirement on exchange rate policy is fairly typical of an area in which Congress takes an interest. Nor is the exchange rate report

---

5. See the list compiled by the Clerk of the House of Representatives (US House of Representatives 2007). Mullen (2006) estimates that 10,000 executive branch reports are received by the Senate alone.

unique in terms of the balance of expertise between Congress and the executive, the sensitivity of financial markets, or the engagement of foreign governments.

It should also be noted that the struggle between Congress and the Treasury over Chinese exchange rate policy, particularly as to whether it constitutes "manipulation," is by no means unique in federal politics. In fact, it is symptomatic of the broader problem of congressional delegation to and influence over the executive branch that is played out across a host of policy areas on a regular basis. Relations between these two branches of government exhibit a well-known set of problems that inhibit the smooth functioning of policy and accountability mechanisms. These include conflicting objectives of the Congress and executive agency, slippage between the preferences of the principal and those of the agent, asymmetries in expertise, collective character of the principal, inconsistent oversight, and agency resistance to disclosure. These difficulties derive ultimately from the constitutional system of separation of powers and checks and balances among the branches of government, as well as from standard problems in the relationship between agents and principals.[6] The pervasiveness of these problems in American government should not lead us to accept weaknesses in exchange rate policy accountability, however. These weaknesses have far-reaching consequences not just for US policy but for the international monetary system. As the recommendations presented in this book will show, we have the means to strengthen accountability. This normative conclusion constitutes another premise of the book.

Congressional delegation to the executive in the area of exchange rates involves third parties—foreign monetary authorities in the case of currency manipulation and exchange rate cooperation, for example— which also characterizes delegation in some other policy areas. Focus on a third party as the target of a congressional mandate complicates the relationship between the Congress (principal) and Treasury (agent). To begin with, negotiations between Treasury and its foreign counterparts might be opaque to Congress, complicating verification that Treasury is faithfully pursuing its mandate. In addition, third parties might readily detect the conflicting preferences between the two branches and maneuver to exploit them. Some observers counsel leaving wide discretion in the hands of the Treasury with respect to its negotiations with China, for example, on the reasoning that constraining the department could block mutually beneficial bargains with Beijing. However, Thomas Schelling (1960) demonstrated long ago that flexibility can also work to a negotia-

---

6. The political science literature on congressional delegation and oversight includes, but is by no means limited to, Aberbach (1990, 2002); Rosenbloom (2000); Epstein and O'Halloran (1994, 1995, 1999); McCubbins and Schwartz (1984); McCubbins, Noll, and Weingast (1987, 1989); and Shepsle (1992).

tor's disadvantage, a finding reinforced by Robert Putnam's analysis of two-level games (Putnam 1988; see also Evans, Jacobson, and Putnam 1993). Following this logic, tightening the accountability of Treasury to Congress could potentially improve the outcomes of negotiations for the United States.

Organization of the Study

Chapter 2 examines the foundations of democratic accountability, that is, the definitions of key terms and debates over the role of the Congress and Treasury in exchange rate policymaking. Chapter 3 surveys the origins and key provisions of the exchange rate sections of the 1988 Act. Chapter 4 examines the treatment of key policy episodes and issues, including but not limited to currency manipulation, in the 35 reports that Treasury has submitted to Congress since 1988. Chapter 5 then examines how Congress has followed up those reports. Chapter 6 presents recommendations, including on how exchange rate provisions should be amended by prospective legislation. Relating these recommendations to democratic governance under globalization, the final chapter concludes the study.

2

Foundations of Accountability

How should the quality of accountability in exchange rate policy be assessed? What litmus tests should be administered? What standards apply?

Definition and Prerequisites

"Accountability," as Ruth Grant and Robert Keohane (2005, 29) define the term, "implies that some actors have the right to hold other actors to a set of standards, to judge whether they have fulfilled their responsibilities in light of these standards, and to impose sanctions if they determine that these responsibilities have not been met." Accountability has several prerequisites: (1) general acceptance (legitimacy) of the right of one actor (the US Treasury in the case of exchange rate policy) to exercise particular authorities and the right of the other (Congress) to hold it to account; (2) standards for assessing whether the power wielder has properly discharged its responsibilities; and (3) sufficient transparency and information to assess whether standards have been fulfilled.

The first prerequisite is satisfied in the United States. The US Constitution gives Congress the power "[t]o coin money, regulate the value thereof, and of foreign coin . . ." (Article I, section 8). Congress delegates the authorities of both the Federal Reserve and Treasury on monetary and exchange rate policies,[1] and both entities are formally accountable to the

---

1. Originally through the Federal Reserve Act of 1913 and the Gold Reserve Act of 1934, respectively. The legislative history of the latter and subsequent amendments to it are discussed by Henning (1999), among others.

legislature across the full range of their responsibilities. The Treasury and Federal Reserve prefer to make and administer exchange rate policy in confidence. Together they constitute the core of a policymaking system that historically has been closed to outside purview and remains veiled relative to many other policy areas (see Destler and Henning 1989).

Treasuries and central banks dominate this policy domain in most other countries as well. Some analysts would prefer that legislatures recuse themselves from currency matters (discussed below). But confidentiality with respect to market operations, which should be preserved, can be distinguished from oversight of these agencies with respect to the basic objectives of policy. Congress's constitutional responsibility to oversee the Treasury and Federal Reserve in the US system is beyond dispute. Its oversight powers are reinforced by its control over grants of authority, appropriations, and appointments to key posts in these agencies—although it has not always used these tools.

The second and third prerequisites in the United States are less complete.

Consider the standards for assessment. In most countries, national legislation that establishes the authorities of the finance ministry and central bank focuses largely on their domestic tasks; their roles in exchange rate policy are usually not completely defined. Under the Bretton Woods regime, the Treasury was directed to maintain the par value for the dollar. After the shift to flexible exchange rates, Treasury was enjoined to use its Exchange Stabilization Fund (ESF) in ways that were simply "[c]onsistent with the obligations of the Government in the International Monetary Fund on orderly exchange arrangements and a stable system of exchange rates" (31 USC 5302b). The Exchange Rates and International Economic Policy Coordination Act of 1988 mandated Treasury to pursue "international economic coordination" where possible and to review the currency practices of trading partners, identify instances of exchange rate manipulation, and pursue negotiations to halt manipulation (discussed in chapter 3). No general statement in legislation sets overall objectives for exchange rate policy and its relationship to domestic monetary and fiscal policies. Therefore, while these mandates set down some specific markers by which Congress can judge Treasury's performance, they are partial, vague in come critical cases, and collectively incomplete.

The reporting provisions of the 1988 Act addressed the third prerequisite—sufficient transparency to hold the authorized officials to account. In the Act, Treasury is required to discuss exchange rate policy in the context of the broader macroeconomic environment and in light of global current account balances and capital movements. The department is directed to provide information and analysis on a formidable list of policy and financial topics. Its reports are evaluated in chapter 4. Congress is by no means limited to information provided by the Treasury; it can of course also draw on the plentiful information available from private-sector financial analysts, independent policy analysts, and private-sector lobbying groups, among other sources. Information regarding policy, policy intentions, and international negotiations, however, is more closely held within the official sector. On this dimension in particular, Congress has not always had sufficient information to exercise effective oversight.

Debate over the Role of Congress

A normative debate exists over the appropriate degree of "democratization" of exchange rate policy despite the legislature's constitutional standing in this area. Several economists are deeply skeptical that Congress can play a constructive role in this policy domain. For example, Kathryn Dominguez and Jeffrey Frankel (1993, 50–53, 137–38), while advocating broader consultation within the executive, oppose a broader role for Congress and more generally a "democratized" exchange rate policy. A broadening of the exchange rate policy process, they fear, could some day induce policymakers to push the exchange rate away from equilibrium rather than toward it. More recently, Jeffrey Frankel and Shang-jin Wei (2007) also are implicitly skeptical of Congress—which they portray as preoccupied with the bilateral trade effects of currency values as opposed to "legitimate economic variables." They absolve the Treasury of protectionism when it has cited countries for manipulation in the past, on the proposition that it was acting under pressure from Congress. Frankel and Wei note with approval that the White House considers a broader set of effects when making policy than does Congress.

I. M. Destler and I (Destler and Henning 1989), by contrast, argue that Congress played a constructive role during the mid-1980s, intermediating between private-sector activism and executive neglect, and helping to produce a needed shift in exchange rate policy by the second Reagan administration. We recommended broadening intra-executive deliberations over the exchange rate, strengthening the role of Congress in setting broad international economic objectives, and institutionalizing and legitimating private-sector advice to the Treasury. The present analysis extends these recommendations, arguing that the experience since the mid-1980s reinforces the case for strengthening the role of Congress in setting objectives and overseeing executive performance in light of these objectives.

Congress has not always behaved consistently in this policy domain. It has sometimes resisted quota increases for the IMF and has imposed multiple, particularistic mandates for the US executive director—but later regretted that the institution was not more aggressive against countries that manipulate currencies. Congress also placed temporary restrictions on Treasury's use of the ESF during fiscal years 1996 and 1997 that were counterproductive. Nonetheless, by and large, Congress has been circumspect on exchange rate policy, limiting its own role in this domain to defining reasonable (though incomplete) objectives, requiring some degree of transparency, and avoiding encroachment on Treasury's operational responsibilities.

To some extent, this disagreement over the role of Congress might reflect differences between the preoccupation of economists with policy optimization, and sometimes a professional preference for technocratic management, and the preoccupation of political scientists with institutional governance, democracy, and accountability. These contrasting approaches will color the debate about delegation, accountability, and oversight as the reform discussion evolves.

Executive Discretion and Congressional Oversight

Treasury holds the "lead" among executive agencies and the Federal Reserve in the exchange rate policy domain. The secretary is the chief financial officer of the US government and represents it on the governing boards of international financial institutions such as the IMF and World Bank. The secretary holds sole discretion over the use of the ESF and is typically the only cabinet member allowed to make public pronouncements on the exchange rate. Senior Treasury officials conduct delicate confidential negotiations with foreign counterparts, such as within the Group of Seven (G-7), in concert with Federal Reserve officials. The Treasury rightly reserves these tasks and should retain a good deal of discretion in carrying them out. Advancing US interests in international monetary policy and cooperation requires a strong Treasury.

The department reports to the Congress, and to the public, on international financial matters through several channels in addition to the biannual exchange rate reports. The Treasury and Federal Reserve issue a joint report quarterly on exchange rates, foreign exchange intervention, and their international reserve holdings.[2] The annual financial statement and monthly balance sheets of the ESF are published with a short lag.[3] Treasury posts the US international reserve position weekly.[4] Any loan agreement involving the ESF is notified within 60 days to the international relations committees of both chambers, as required by the Case Act.

---

2. See, for example, Federal Reserve Bank of New York, "Treasury and Federal Reserve Foreign Exchange Operations," November 8, 2007, available at www.newyorkfed.org (accessed March 19, 2008).

3. See, for example, Department of Treasury, Office of the Inspector General, "Audit Report," available at www.treas.gov (accessed March 19, 2008).

4. See, for example, US International Reserve Position, released December 17, 2007, available at www.treas.gov (accessed March 19, 2008).

This list is not exhaustive.[5] Some of these reports, particularly the quarterly joint report with the Federal Reserve, overlap the coverage of those mandated by the 1988 Act. However, none of the reports just listed offer statements of policy or substantial analysis, which are mandated by the exchange rate provisions of that Act.

Congress's treatment of these reports and indeed its oversight more broadly sustain a list of criticisms by the executive and independent agencies and advocates of accountability generally. First of all, Congress sometimes mandates and then ignores reports by executive agencies; its attention to certain issues can be cyclical or episodic. Second, Congress is fragmented by its separation into two chambers and by the committee structure within each. The division of labor by committee leads to questions of jurisdiction and serious problems of intercommittee coordination. Committees can compete with one another on oversight—leading, for example, to excessive demands for testimony on salient policy issues—and on legislation. The Congress was not designed primarily to be an efficient institution, and dysfunctionalities in accountability can arise from its weaknesses. The answer to these criticisms is not to weaken congressional oversight, but rather to address its flaws in order to strengthen the accountability process.

It is nonetheless worth specifying the pitfalls that Congress should avoid in delegating to the Treasury in the area of exchange rate policy. First, it would be inappropriate for Congress to mandate to Treasury objectives that were not possible to meet, either because they were conflicting or because the department did not possess the relevant instruments. Given that exchange rates and international monetary policy are subject to multiple pressures, private and official, the injunction against unrealistic mandates is important. It would be inappropriate, for example, for Congress to mandate pursuit of an exchange rate or current account target that was inconsistent with the legislature's own fiscal choices or the Federal Reserve's monetary policy. Second, while Congress can mandate objectives, it would be inappropriate for the legislature to mandate an outcome to international negotiations that depended in turn on the willingness of foreign governments to cooperate. Third, deflecting politically unpopular decisions to executive agencies and then criticizing them—scapegoating—may be common, but it is also inappropriate.

Potential conflict between maintaining room for maneuver for Treasury and the accountability mechanism arises in two ways. First, accountability sometimes deliberately restricts the agent's discretion, as the 1988 Act sought to do with respect to currency manipulation. Second, disclosure of information necessary to conduct oversight can potentially undercut

---

5. Congress also mandated a set of separate reports from Treasury after the Mexican peso crisis of 1994–95 and the Asian financial crisis of 1997–98.

Treasury's effectiveness if, for example, foreign interlocutors wish to preserve confidentiality. However, international norms have evolved toward substantially increased transparency since the 1988 Act was drafted, and accountability mechanisms can be designed to minimize (though perhaps not eliminate) the tradeoff with policy effectiveness.

As a matter of principle, the more authority and autonomy is delegated to an agency, the more important are reporting, disclosure, and oversight. Delegation and accountability go hand in hand. It is appropriate for Congress to set broad policy goals, and some specific ones, and to insist that Treasury provide information and defend its use of discretion. Rather than inhibiting good performance by the Treasury, disclosure requirements and other mechanisms that give Congress continuing influence over the policy agenda can best be seen as preconditions for extensive prior delegation to the department.[6]

---

6. This argument is developed generally in Epstein and O'Halloran (1994).

3

The Exchange Rates and International Economic Policy Coordination Act of 1988

As a prelude to examining the usefulness of the exchange rate reporting process, a review is in order of the origins of the Exchange Rates and International Economic Policy Coordination Act of 1988 and its key elements. This legislation is reproduced in appendix A. It was passed as part of the much larger, and better known, Omnibus Trade and Competitiveness Act of 1988.

Origins

The 1988 Act was forged in the heat of the international trade and monetary conflicts of the mid-1980s. During the early part of that decade, the United States pursued a combination of loose fiscal policy and tight monetary policy that came to be called the "Reagan-Volcker" policy mix. The mix produced an appreciation of the dollar and trade and current account deficits that set new records. Rather than alter domestic macroeconomic policy in light of these external consequences, the first Reagan administration actively encouraged capital inflows to finance the fiscal and current account deficits. These policies produced a flood of imports and pressure on traded goods producers that was unprecedented in the postwar period. When these interest groups complained to the US Treasury, Secretary Donald T. Regan and his Undersecretary for International Affairs, Beryl W. Sprinkel, told them that Treasury would not attempt to cap the value of the dollar for their benefit. These groups then brought their complaints to Congress.[1]

Congress responded in three ways. First, a number of committees held hearings on the issue, raising public consciousness and building a case for policy action. Second, several members proposed trade legislation that would favor domestic industry. Resentment of the administration's trade policy ran so deep that one protrade member claimed, hyperbolically, that the House of Representatives would have passed the Smoot-Hawley bill had it been brought to the floor during the summer of 1985. Third, members of Congress proposed legislation that would require the Treasury and Federal Reserve to address the exchange rate.

Such legislation went through two phases. The first set of bills would have required these agencies to intervene in the foreign exchange market in prescribed amounts to depress the value of the dollar. These bills were impractical, but they forced the administration to take the sentiments of the Congress on this issue seriously. The chairman of the Ways and Means Committee, Dan Rostenkowski (D-IL), proposed an "exchange rate equalization tariff" directed at newly industrialized economies (NIEs) that maintained undervalued currencies—a precursor to similar bills before the present Congress. The second set of bills endeavored to make the executive more accountable with respect to exchange rate and related policy, more responsive when a broad set of private interests object to the value of the dollar, and more vigilant with respect to specific countries that maintained undervalued rates.

During 1985, James A. Baker III, who had replaced Donald Regan as secretary of the Treasury at the outset of the second Reagan administration, addressed the issue by launching the process that resulted in the Plaza Accord of September of that year and the Louvre Accord of February 1987. This process produced—or, depending on one's view of the effectiveness of government action in this domain, contributed to—a dramatic depreciation of the dollar and then a partial stabilization. It was coupled by an effort, more effective in some cases than in others, to alter monetary and fiscal policies among partners as well as at home to contribute to the adjustment of current account imbalances (see Funabashi 1988, Frankel 1995). Baker's actions bought time and some goodwill on Capitol Hill, which allowed the administration to defang some of the more protectionist elements from what was to become the Omnibus Trade and Competitiveness Act of 1988. However, a number of currencies, notably the New Taiwan dollar and the Korean won, remained undervalued even as they appreciated in bilateral nominal terms against the US dollar, given the dollar's depreciation against the yen and European

---

1. For a review of this episode, see Destler and Henning (1989); Henning (1994); and Destler (2005).

currencies.[2] So the sponsors of the 1988 Act sought, among several other things, to appreciate such undervalued currencies as well as to prevent a repeat of the policies of the first Reagan administration.

The drafters of the exchange rate legislation looked to the IMF's Articles of Agreement for a statement of members' obligations with respect to exchange rates. Article IV states in part, "In particular, each member shall . . . avoid manipulating exchange rates or the international monetary system in order to prevent effective balance of payments adjustment or to gain an unfair competitive advantage over other members. . . ." This passage, introduced with the second amendment to the Articles of Agreement after the transition to floating exchange rates in the 1970s, provided the basis for special consultations with Sweden in 1982 and Korea in 1987 when their policies became suspect. However, the Fund has never cited a member for manipulation. The Executive Board had established guidelines that Fund staff were to follow in surveillance of members' exchange rate policies, including specific criteria that could indicate proscribed manipulation (Article IV and the 1977 guidelines, as amended through June 2007, are reproduced in appendices B and C, respectively).[3] For the section of the 1988 Act that addressed the currency policies of the East Asian NIEs, the drafters borrowed heavily from the language of Article IV.

Key Elements

The 1988 Act contains six sections, 3001 to 3006, devoted respectively to short title, findings, statement of policy, international negotiations, reporting requirements, and definitions.[4]

In section 3002, Congress found that patterns of exchange rates contributed to trade and current account imbalances, and that this was true in particular of the appreciation of the dollar during the early 1980s, "imposing serious strains on the world trading system and frustrating both business and government planning." Currency manipulation on the part of some "major trading nations" continued to create "serious" competitive problems for US industry. A "more stable exchange rate" at a level consistent with "a more appropriate and sustainable" balance in the current account should be "a major focus of national economic policy." Macroeconomic policy coordination and foreign exchange intervention could be useful tools to that end.

---

2. See C. Fred Bergsten, statement before the Hearing on Currency Manipulation, Subcommittee on International Trade, Committee on Finance, United States Senate, Washington, May 12, 1989. See also Balassa and Williamson (1990).

3. See also Goldstein (2006) and Mussa (2007).

4. The Act is reproduced in appendix A.

Section 3003 states that "[i]t is the policy of the United States that" the United States and its partners should continue the process of coordinating "monetary, fiscal, and structural policies" begun with the Plaza Accord. The goal of the United States in international economic negotiations should be "to achieve macroeconomic policies and exchange rates consistent with more appropriate and sustainable balances in trade and capital flows and to foster price stability in conjunction with economic growth." The United States and its partners should intervene, "in combination with necessary macroeconomic policy changes," to bring this about. While recognizing that the exchange rate and balance of payments were embedded in a broader macroeconomic framework, Congress intended for the exchange rate and the level of foreign borrowing to become matters of conscious policy (US Congress 1988, 84). The section adds, pointedly, that "the accountability of the President for the impact of economic policies and exchange rates on trade competitiveness should be increased."

Section 3004 addresses two levels of negotiations: (1) multilateral, where the president is directed to "seek to confer and negotiate" to achieve these objectives; and (2) bilateral, the heart of the antimanipulation provisions. Under the bilateral negotiations subsection, the Act directs the secretary of the Treasury to "analyze on an annual basis" the exchange rate policies of other countries for evidence of manipulation against the dollar "for purposes of preventing effective balance of payments adjustments or gaining unfair competitive advantage in international trade." This language adhered deliberately, though not exactly, to Article IV of the IMF Articles of Agreement and, like that article, did not define "manipulation" further. (Within the IMF, guidance on this definition was provided in principles that were adopted by a decision of the Executive Board, as discussed below.)

The secretary is to apply a three-part test. If a country (1) manipulates its rate, (2) runs "material global current account surpluses," and (3) has "significant bilateral trade surpluses with the United States," then the secretary "shall take action to initiate negotiations with such foreign countries on an expedited basis" in the Fund or bilaterally, to ensure that the cited country "regularly and promptly" adjusts its exchange rate to eliminate the unfair advantage and permit balance of payments adjustment. These negotiations will likely produce results only with the assent of foreign counterparts. Legislation can require only that the secretary approach counterparts for negotiations, but if the negotiations yield little, the secretary is expected to explain.

Notably, the secretary is not required to initiate negotiations in cases where they would have a "serious detrimental impact on vital national economic and security interests," but would have to inform the chairpersons and ranking members of the banking committees of both houses of such a determination. This waiver, however, does not relieve the Treasury of a finding of manipulation when circumstances dictate, only of the requirement to pursue negotiations once manipulation is found.

Section 3005 details the reporting requirements. The secretary of the Treasury shall submit a report annually to the banking committees of both houses, on or before October 15, with written six-month updates (on April 15). The department shall consult with the Federal Reserve when preparing the report. The secretary shall testify to the banking committees on the report if requested to do so. The section originally also directed the Federal Reserve, for its part, to analyze the impact of the dollar's exchange rate on the US economy in its semiannual Humphrey-Hawkins reports to Congress—a provision that survived, albeit in amended form, the revision to the Federal Reserve's monetary policy reporting mandate in 2000.[5]

The section specifies a long list of information that Treasury must include in its reports:

- "an analysis of currency market developments" and exchange rates;

- an evaluation of the determinants of exchange rates;

- "a description of currency intervention" and other exchange market actions;

- assessment of the impact of the dollar's exchange rate on the "competitive performance" of "industries," trade and current account balances, production, growth, employment, and external indebtedness;

- recommendations for "any changes in United States economic policy to attain a more appropriate and sustainable" current account balance;

- the results of negotiations over currency manipulation;

- issues arising in Article IV consultations with the IMF; and

- a report on international capital flows and their effects.

The 1988 Act thus placed a substantial additional burden on the Treasury to collect, analyze, and report these assessments to Congress. In passing this legislation, members of Congress expected Treasury to convey analytical substance that would provide a foundation for meaningful oversight. They also intended that these reports inform the broader public discourse on international economic policy and the external ramifications of domestic monetary and fiscal policies. Above all, they wanted to make it more difficult for Treasury to neglect a strong dollar and undervalued foreign currencies as it had under Secretary Regan. Treasury did not need this legislation to combat currency manipulation on the part of foreign

---

5. Federal Reserve Act, Section 2B, as amended December 27, 2000, available at www.federal reserve.gov (accessed March 19, 2008).

governments; it had the authority and ability already. The legislation was an effort by members of Congress to provide greater leverage to the department's bargaining position and to prod Treasury to act against manipulation when it might not otherwise do so.

Comparison with IMF Language

There are two important differences between the language of the IMF's Article IV and exchange rate surveillance guidelines, on the one hand, and the United States' 1988 Act, on the other. First, the IMF language is formally symmetrical with respect to overvaluation and undervaluation. Although the IMF staff's interpretation of Article IV emphasized intent to prevent adjustment, which compromised the Fund's ability to enforce manipulation in both directions, countries were in principle enjoined against manipulating the rate to achieve either (IMF 2006, 15; Frankel and Wei 2007). Under the 1988 Act, the designation for manipulation is also symmetrical in principle. But the Treasury is mandated to pursue negotiations only with countries that "(1) have material global current account surpluses; and (2) have significant bilateral trade surpluses with the United States." Negotiations are not mandated for countries running trade and current account deficits. In addition, whereas the IMF focuses on overall current account surpluses, the US legislation also introduces the bilateral trade balance and directs Treasury to consider both. While acknowledging the bilateral balance as politically salient, a large majority of economists regard it as a policy-irrelevant concept in a world of multilateral trade (Noland 1997, Frankel and Wei 2007).

4

Review of the Reports

The US Treasury has submitted 35 reports during the nearly 20 years since the Exchange Rates and International Economic Policy Coordination Act of 1988. The reports might be assessed by at least three standards. The narrowest test would be whether the reports meet the content requirements of the 1988 Act. A second test would be whether the reports provide the basis for informed oversight by Congress, including information that is not already openly available or at least has value added by virtue of its presentation or analysis. The broadest test would ask whether the reports address policies and problems that the markets, the public, and Congress care about.

This book is concerned with all three standards, so this chapter takes a broad approach and examines the reports' treatment of important questions confronting international monetary policy in general: early findings of manipulation, the Mexican peso crisis of 1994–95, the Asian financial crisis of 1997–98, the Economic and Monetary Union (EMU) in Europe, Japanese intervention in 2003–04, fiscal policy, and Chinese exchange rate policy during 2000–07. The chapter finds that, while the reports technically satisfy most of the content requirements of the 1988 Act, they are incomplete as a basis for oversight and often overlook major policy questions.

Appendix table 4A.1 provides a comprehensive overview and summary of the Treasury reports. Figures 4.1a and 4.1b present the exchange rate of the dollar against the Deutsche mark/euro and the Japanese yen over the period, respectively, while figure 4.2 shows the nominal and real effective rate of the dollar and figure 4.3 presents the US current account balance.

Findings of Manipulation, 1988–94

In its first report, in October 1988, the Treasury Department found that Korea and Taiwan manipulated their exchange rates and announced that it would initiate negotiations with those countries. Both governments had resisted the rise of their currencies against the dollar and allowed only modest appreciations in real effective terms after the Plaza Accord (figures 4.4a and 4.4b). C. Fred Bergsten and then Assistant Secretary of the Treasury for International Affairs David C. Mulford had advocated appreciation of these currencies in 1986 and 1987, respectively, supported by analysis by Bela Balassa and John Williamson (1987, 1990). By 1988, these countries showed large increases in current account and bilateral trade surpluses. (See figures 4.5a and 4.5b for current account balances and figures 4.6a and 4.6b for trade balances.) They also maintained capital and exchange controls.[1]

Treasury's formal designation of Korea and Taiwan for manipulation came at a time when the United States was pressing trade partners for market access quite aggressively. One instrument being used toward that end was the separate provision of the Omnibus Trade and Competitiveness Act of 1988 called "Super 301." It is worth noting that congressional oversight hearings directly linked the exchange rate and Super 301 negotiations (US Senate 1989). Pressure on trade policy strengthened Treasury's bargaining position on exchange rate matters. Both countries also had an unusual relationship with the United States on military security, and neither could afford to jeopardize those ties. Accordingly, both Korea and Taiwan acceded to negotiations and allowed further modest appreciation of their currencies against the dollar after the October 1988 report (figures 4.4a and 4.4b).[2]

Taiwan had run an overall current account surplus of 18.5 percent of GNP in 1987 and, although appreciation that year improved the bilateral trade deficit during 1988, the New Taiwan dollar had not appreciated during January–September 1988, and Treasury expected Taiwan's external surpluses to reemerge (figure 4.5b). When citing Taiwan, Treasury also noted capital and exchange controls, particularly on capital inflows,

---

1. In testimony to the Senate Finance Committee in the spring of 1989, Bergsten and Williamson criticized the manipulation designation, arguing that by then the appreciation of the New Taiwan dollar and the Korean won had been sufficient to produce adjustment. See C. Fred Bergsten, statement before the Hearing on Currency Manipulation, Subcommittee on International Trade, Committee on Finance, United States Senate, Washington, May 12, 1989; and John Williamson, statement on exchange rate policy in Hong Kong, Korea, and Taiwan before the Hearing on Currency Manipulation, Subcommittee on International Trade, Committee on Finance, United States Senate, Washington, May 12, 1989. See also GAO (1989).

2. Kim (1993) and Wang (1993) argue that US pressure was important in producing this outcome. See also Mo and Myers (1993).

Figure 4.1a   Exchange rate of US dollar against Deutsche mark/euro, January 1988–December 2007

Deutsche mark/euro per US dollar

Source: PACIFIC Exchange Rate Service, available at http://fx.sauder.ubc.ca.

Figure 4.1b   Exchange rate of US dollar against Japanese yen, January 1988–December 2007

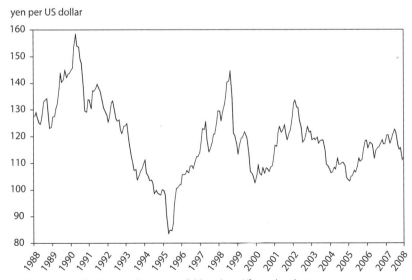

yen per US dollar

Source: PACIFIC Exchange Rate Service, available at http://fx.sauder.ubc.ca.

**Figure 4.2   Nominal and real effective exchange rate of US dollar,
January 1988–October 2007**

index (June 2000 = 100)

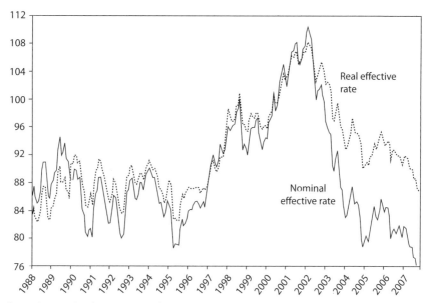

Source: International Monetary Fund, *International Financial Statistics*, various years.

and large amounts of intervention. In response, Taiwanese authorities reformed their exchange rate system in April 1989 and allowed a 12 percent appreciation between October 1988 and October 1989. The bilateral trade deficit fell, but remained the largest among the Asian newly industrialized economies (NIEs) for some time (see figures 4.6a, 4.6b, and 4.6c). In its October 1989 report, nonetheless, Treasury declared that there was no further need for appreciation at that time and delisted Taiwan as a manipulator (US Treasury reports, October 1988, April 1989, October 1989).

In March 1990, the Korean government announced a change in its exchange rate regime, leading the US Treasury to remove the manipulation designation in the April 1990 report. While Treasury justified the removal by the liberalization of the foreign exchange market in Korea, the shift also coincided with the disappearance of Korea's current account surplus (see Frankel 1992).

Treasury nonetheless expressed its concern that both governments retained the ability to manipulate the exchange rate, noted that the currency should continue to contribute to adjustment of their external balances, and warned that it would continue to scrutinize the policies of both countries. In fact, the department relisted Taiwan in the May 1992 report,

Figure 4.3   US current account balance, 1988–2007

billions of dollars

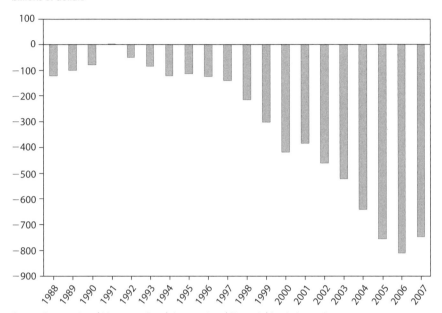

Source: International Monetary Fund, *International Financial Statistics*, various years.

maintained the designation in the following report, and delisted the country again in May 1993.

China is treated for the first time in the November 1990 Treasury report, which noted that China had been running overall current account and trade deficits during most of the previous decade, but that its bilateral trade surpluses with the United States had been growing since 1985 (figure 4.6c). Although China had an administered foreign exchange system that was used to support exports, the principal cause of the bilateral imbalance was general administrative controls over trade.[3] China was not yet cited as a manipulator.

During the two subsequent reports, Treasury ratcheted up its analysis of the Chinese exchange rate system and its warnings to Beijing. The May 1991 report noted that China's overall current account balance shifted from deficit in 1989 to significant surplus in 1990 (figure 4.5c). In

3. In a passage that foreshadowed the economic diplomacy of the mid-2000s, Treasury said, "It is a matter of concern for the United States Government. There is, thus, an interagency effort to formulate a strategy for addressing this problem. Moreover, we aim to press China through any available bilateral contact and in the international financial institutions (especially the IMF and World Bank) to remove its restrictions" (US Treasury report, November 1990, 31).

Figure 4.4a   Korean won per US dollar, end of period, January 1986–December 1994

won per US dollar

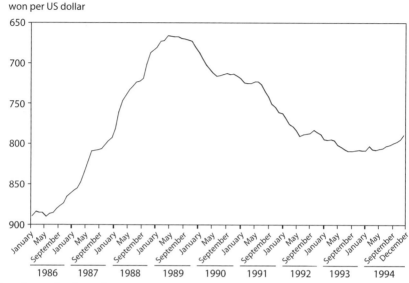

Note: Inverted scale applies.

Source: International Monetary Fund, *International Financial Statistics*, various years.

Figure 4.4b   New Taiwan dollar per US dollar, end of period, January 1986–December 1994

New Taiwan dollar per US dollar

Note: Inverted scale applies.

Source: Central Bank of Republic of China (Taiwan).

Figure 4.4c   Renminbi–US dollar principal exchange rate, end of period, January 1986–December 1994

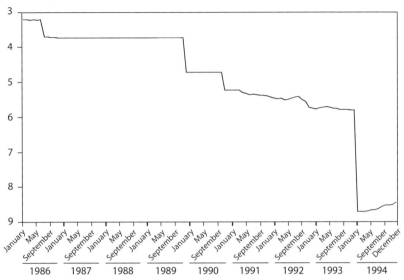

renminbi per US dollar

Note: Inverted scale applies. Prior to the dismantling of the dual exchange rate system in January 1994, the large majority of China's international trade was conducted at exchange rates markedly lower than the official rate shown in this figure, rendering the apparent devaluation at that time somewhat misleading.

Source: International Monetary Fund, *International Financial Statistics*, various years.

the November 1991 report, a quarter of which was devoted to China alone, Treasury announced that its officials had visited that country during the previous July and September to discuss these matters and to "seek concrete steps toward a more market-oriented system of exchange rate determination." While there was "no clear evidence that the authorities manipulate the exchange rate itself," the department remained "seriously concerned" about the size of China's external surpluses.

Treasury finally cited China for manipulation in the May 1992 report. It noted that the renminbi had depreciated in real terms during the previous two to three years in the face of growing external surpluses. (The nominal exchange rate is presented in figure 4.4c.) The rate was closely managed through the administered system, and foreign reserves were rising. Treasury thus concluded that Chinese authorities employed exchange rate policy, in addition to trade controls, to attain competitive advantage in international trade, justifying the designation as a "manipulator" (p. 32). Treasury asked China to take three specific steps: (1) eliminate the foreign exchange surrender system, (2) loosen controls on the swap centers, and (3) make foreign exchange laws and regulations more transparent (p. 33).

Figure 4.5a   Current account balance of Korea, 1986Q1–94Q4

millions of US dollars

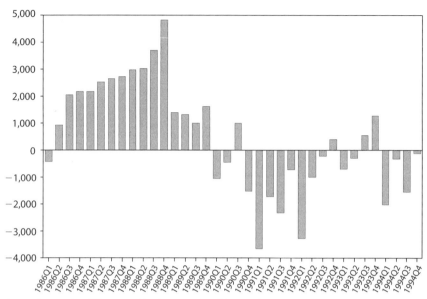

Source: International Monetary Fund, *International Financial Statistics*, various years.

Figure 4.5b   Current account balance of Taiwan, 1986Q1–94Q4

millions of US dollars

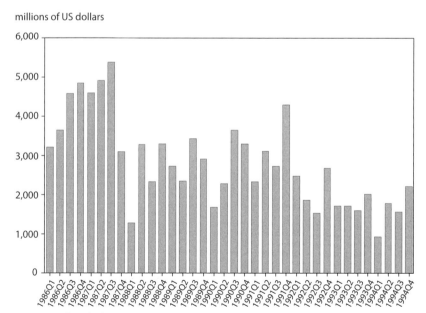

Source: Central Bank of Republic of China (Taiwan).

Figure 4.5c   Current account balance of China, 1986–94

millions of US dollars

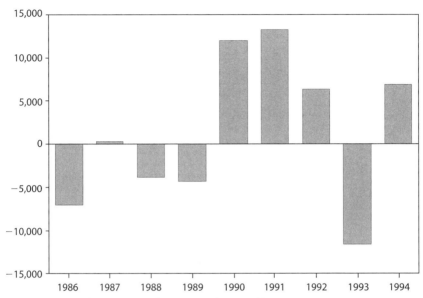

Source: International Monetary Fund, *International Financial Statistics*, various years.

The report also mentioned that China was the subject of a Super 301 trade investigation.

Subsequent reports mention at least four negotiations with Chinese authorities over their exchange rate system. The November 1993 report noted China's application to accede to the World Trade Organization (WTO) but declared, "China has not yet brought its foreign exchange regime into conformity with GATT Article XV," and urged China to do so. At the beginning of 1994, China unified its dual exchange system and introduced other liberalizing reforms. While welcoming these moves, Treasury objected to exclusion of foreign firms from the new interbank market in foreign exchange. Treasury nonetheless removed its manipulation designation in the December 1994 report. The operative passage is worth quoting:

> It is therefore Treasury's determination that China is not currently manipulating its exchange system to prevent effective balance of payments adjustment and gain unfair competitive advantage in international trade, but that it retains the capacity and bureaucratic means to do so in the future. (p. 26)

Treasury reported continued talks with Chinese authorities on these matters through the December 1995 report and occasionally during 1997 and 2001. Despite a steadily rising bilateral trade deficit with China,

Figure 4.6a   US-Korea trade balance, 1986Q1–94Q4

millions of US dollars

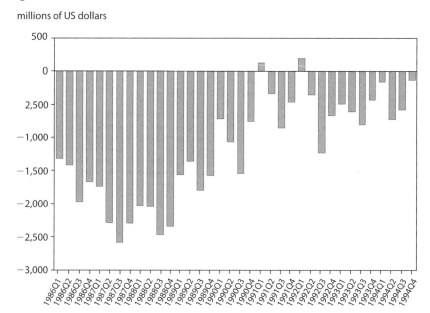

Source: US Census Bureau, Foreign Trade Division, Data Dissemination Branch, available at www.census.gov.

Figure 4.6b   US-Taiwan trade balance, 1986Q1–94Q4

millions of US dollars

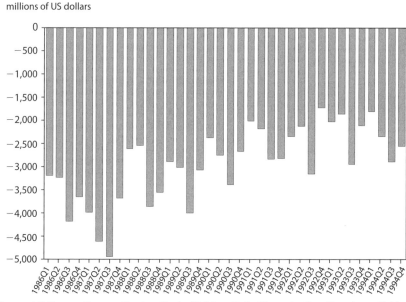

Source: US Census Bureau, Foreign Trade Division, Data Dissemination Branch, available at www.census.gov.

Figure 4.6c   US-China trade balance, 1986Q1–94Q4

millions of US dollars

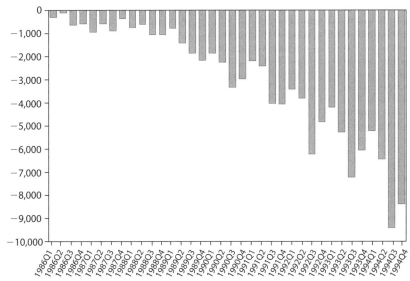

Source: US Census Bureau, Foreign Trade Division, Data Dissemination Branch, available at www.census.gov.

Treasury declined to cite China for manipulation. Although several countries have been reviewed, no other country has been cited in these reports for manipulating its currency since then.

Nicholas Lardy (1994, 86–90, 137) criticized Treasury's manipulation designation, arguing that the effect of Chinese authorities' foreign exchange operations prior to the unification of the dual exchange system in 1994 was to prevent rather than foster further depreciation of the swap market rate. Treasury failed to distinguish between important categories of foreign exchange reserves—those held by the central authorities and those held in state-owned banks and controlled by numerous trading firms—and to recognize that large net outflows of capital, not intervention, placed downward pressure on the renminbi during 1992 and 1993. In other words, Lardy concluded, China's "manipulation" had the opposite effect on the exchange rate of that suggested by Treasury.[4]

What factors explain Treasury's decisions to cite countries for manipulating their currencies in these reports? Why did Treasury cite only

---

4. Lardy added that if China moved toward convertibility on the capital account as well as the current account, as Treasury was urging, Treasury should expect the renminbi to depreciate, not appreciate, in real terms. Note, though, that Treasury later made a clear distinction between determining manipulation and determining undervaluation, which it argued was not required by the 1988 Act. See GAO (2005).

China, Korea, and Taiwan and not others? The extensive use of exchange controls to manage the exchange rate and external trade is a factor common to all of these decisions on manipulation and is consistent with the timing of delisting. Treasury repeatedly referred to controls in the early reports and used this criterion as part of the justification for not citing China in the mid-2000s. External surpluses on the current account and bilateral trade, which are specifically listed in the 1988 Act as criteria for initiating negotiations, are also common to these three cases but do not explain the timing of China's delisting. Finally, all of these countries were important in the international trading system and had attracted attention on Capitol Hill. These factors appear to be Treasury's dominant considerations in deciding which countries should be cited and when.[5]

In a useful paper, Frankel and Wei (2007) test alternative explanations for Treasury's decisions against data for a broad set of US trading partners, including countries that were not cited for manipulation. They find that a country's overall current account balance and an undervalued currency increase the chances that Treasury will review it for manipulation, launch discussions with it, or actually cite it for manipulation. But they stress that the bilateral trade balance, as well as the US unemployment rate, are the more important determinants of Treasury manipulation decisions. They add that in this way, Korea, Taiwan, and China have been "scapegoats" in US policymaking. They do not specifically test the explanatory power of the maintenance of exchange controls.

Finally, it is worth noting that, at least with respect to exchange rate manipulation on the part of the NIEs, Treasury embraced the spirit and letter of the 1988 Act during these early years. Treasury officials appeared pleased to testify on their progress before the banking committees. Undersecretary David C. Mulford, who had opposed stronger versions of the Act before passage, praised the reporting process and stressed the importance of cooperation with Congress. Secretary Nicholas F. Brady called the reporting process "an enormously useful vehicle" (Destler and Henning 1989, 113–14).

Mexican Peso Crisis of 1994–95

During the mid-1990s, Mexico was the third largest trading partner of the United States, and as a neighbor it was also important to a host of other US foreign policy goals. The North American Free Trade Agreement (NAFTA), negotiated by the George H. W. Bush administration and passed by Congress during the Bill Clinton administration, had been the most widely debated trade measure in the United States since World War II.

---

5. See also the tabulation of rationales in GAO (2005, appendix III).

The Mexican peso crisis of 1994–95 threatened political support in the United States for this agreement, and Congress was called upon to fund the largest-ever financial rescue package. Once the worst of the crisis had passed, Congress intensively scrutinized Treasury policymaking with respect to the peso-dollar rate.

The period leading up to the crisis illustrates Treasury's conflicted position. Privately, Treasury officials became increasingly concerned about the viability of Mexico's exchange rate regime. The flow of confidential memoranda, released by members of Congress after investigating the crisis, documents growing alarm in the Treasury and Federal Reserve over Mexican exchange rate policy.[6] However, as financial markets became increasingly concerned about political and economic events in Mexico over the course of 1994, Clinton administration officials continued to publicly express confidence in the Mexican economy.[7]

Accordingly, Treasury's exchange rate reports held no warning of the peso crisis. Despite Mexico's importance to US trade and the substantial amount of time Treasury officials had devoted to the peso problem, there was no significant treatment of Mexico in the department's reports either before or after the crisis. Perhaps neither the manipulation provisions (section 3004(b)) nor the report content provisions (section 3005(b)) strictly required such a discussion. But a forthcoming treatment of international monetary developments of primary concern to the country that went beyond the specific requirements of the law could certainly have included discussion of the peso.

---

6. See US Treasury Department, "Bi-Weekly Report on Mexico," February 15, 1994, Treasury document no. 003280; "Memorandum to Summers and Shafer," March 24, 1994, Treasury document no. 002438; "Memorandum from Summers to Bentsen," April 26, 1994, Treasury document no. 003247-003253; "Memorandum from Geithner to Summers and Shafer: Mexico: Planning for the Next Stage," December 5, 1994, Treasury document no. 001209-210; "Memorandum to Geithner, Summers, and Shafer: Contact the Mexicans Before They Do Something," December 19, 1994, Treasury document no. 702690; "Memorandum from C. Pigott to Bennett: The Mexican Peso," June 3, 1994, Federal Reserve Bank of New York document no. 10003817-19, no. 94-81; Federal Reserve Board, "Memorandum from Siegman to Greenspan and Blinder," August 19, 1994; Kamin and Morton, "The Implied Probability of a Peso Devaluation," August 19, 1994, Federal Reserve Board document no. 94-119; and Kamin and Howard, "Options for Mexican Exchange Rate Policy," August 17, 1994, Federal Reserve Board document no. 94-115.

7. On March 24, 1994, Treasury Secretary Lloyd Bentsen issued a statement that "we have every confidence that Mexico is on the right economic path" (Reuters World Service, March 24, 1994). On November 21, 1994, after billions of dollars had fled the country, Bentsen stated that, "I have been impressed by Mexico's strong economic fundamentals, with falling inflation, stronger growth and a balanced budget. . ." (Memorandum from Summers to Bentsen, "Statement on Mexico," November 21, 1994). In December 1994, with the Mexican economy at a breaking point, President Clinton, at the Miami Summit of the Americas, cited Mexico as a model of successful economic development (Weekly Compilation of Presidential Documents, December 19, 1994).

After the crisis broke in December 1994, the Clinton administration proposed a $40 billion loan guarantee for Mexico to Congress. When Congress refused to act, notwithstanding bipartisan leadership support for the guarantees, Treasury officials announced that they would instead lend up to $20 billion from the Exchange Stabilization Fund (ESF) as part of an international package that included up to $17.8 billion from the IMF (Henning 1999; Rubin and Weisberg 2003).

Feeling circumvented by the use of the ESF, members of Congress launched an investigation into administration policymaking prior to the crisis and into the loan package, holding multiple hearings in several committees (see US Senate 1995). Although Treasury officials testified, this did not satisfy members of Congress. The Mexican Debt Disclosure Act of 1995, passed in April, required Treasury to report in extensive detail on its financial support to Mexico (see Henning 1999, 66–70). The department did so separately from its exchange rate reports (US Treasury 1995a, 1995b, 1996). Senator Alfonse D'Amato (R-NY), who as chairman of the Senate Banking Committee was particularly active, used the legislative budget process to attach temporary restrictions on Treasury's use of the ESF. In the final analysis, Treasury's financial support for Mexico was a success, and the D'Amato restrictions were counterproductive (Henning 1999, 66–70). But the backlash against Treasury policy highlights the political consequences of presenting Congress with unpleasant surprises.

This episode generates several observations. First, the manipulation provisions of the 1988 Act do not mandate negotiations in cases of overvaluation; they are asymmetrical. Second, the peso crisis demonstrates that overvalued currencies can pose as much risk to the US economy as undervalued currencies. However, in contrast to the cases of undervaluation in East Asia during 1988–94, Treasury did not find the reports to be a useful vehicle to cajole Mexico toward greater exchange rate flexibility. Third, one might nonetheless ask whether the congressional backlash would have been muted if Treasury had given the peso more attention in these reports prior to the crisis. Exiting from an overvalued peg risks greater financial disruption than exiting from an undervalued one, and Treasury would have to be cautious. But that does not necessarily mean that Treasury can say nothing useful publicly in such cases in the future.[8]

Asian Financial Crisis of 1997–98

The crisis that swept across East Asia, extending to Russia and Latin America, dominated international financial policy during the second half

---

8. Goldstein (1997, 59–62) argues that a middle ground between saying nothing and causing a currency crisis, narrow as it might be, exists in the case of the IMF. As argued below, similar reasoning applies to Treasury reports.

of the 1990s. US Treasury officials worked on this problem intensively, bilaterally, and in cooperation with G-7 partners and the IMF, issuing a number of important statements and testifying frequently on Capitol Hill (see US House of Representatives 1997, 1998a). Remarkably, however, Treasury suspended its exchange rate reports to the Congress. Distracted by weekly financial firefights and unwilling to telegraph their intentions to the markets, Treasury officials evidently saw little benefit in these reports to their handling of the crises.

When it finally released its report in January 1999, Treasury pinned much of the blame for the crisis on the weakness of domestic financial systems in the stricken countries. It urged Japan and its banks to clean up the financial system and duly reported intervention in June 1998 to support the yen, then at around 146 to the dollar. Treasury had also improved the format and readability of the statement, which thereafter stylistically resembled a JPMorgan or Goldman Sachs brief on the exchange markets.

The report cited no country for manipulating its exchange rate. Under the leadership of Secretary Robert Rubin and Deputy Secretary Lawrence Summers, in an effort to make the definition of manipulation more systematic and transparent, the Treasury had listed four criteria in its December 1995 report (pp. 11–13)—external balances, exchange restrictions and capital controls, exchange rate movements, and movements in reserves—and in its February 1997 report added a fifth criterion, macroeconomic trends. Although China had a record and growing current account surplus, a growing bilateral trade surplus with the United States, and controls on capital inflows, and had intervened to prevent appreciation of the renminbi, the January 1999 report cited a slowdown in growth—the newest criterion—when concluding that China had not manipulated its currency.

Japanese Yen

The dollar's rate against the Japanese yen had been one of the causes of the politicization of exchange rate policy during the mid-1980s and a motive for the 1988 Act. During most of the period covered by the reports, the Japanese economy was mired in prolonged stagnation, a consequence of the bursting of the asset bubble at the end of the 1980s. The yen-dollar rate reemerged as a political issue periodically, first under Clinton's first Treasury secretary, Lloyd Bentsen, second as the Japanese currency appreciated to a record 80 to the dollar in mid-1995, and third when it weakened to (nearly) 150 to the dollar in 1998 (figure 4.1b). The Treasury and Federal Reserve intervened in the yen-dollar foreign exchange market during these episodes and reported these operations accordingly (see US Treasury reports of April 1989, 9; October 1989, 8; August 1995, 12–13;

and December 1995, 2–4). With the exception of brief statements that intervention was effective, the treatment in the exchange rate reports was largely descriptive rather than analytical and largely duplicated the report on foreign currency operations provided in the *Federal Reserve Bulletin*.

The Great Intervention of 2003–04 represents a fourth politically salient episode involving the yen. During this period, just as their economy was emerging from its prolonged slump, Japanese authorities purchased $320 billion to restrain the appreciation of the yen from about 120 at the beginning of 2003 to about 108 at the end of that year. US Treasury officials suspended their objections to intervention in principle in the belief that intervention would facilitate a monetary expansion in Japan that would help to sustain its recovery. As massive interventions continued, however, Undersecretary for International Affairs John B. Taylor insisted that his Japanese counterparts develop an "exit strategy," which they implemented in March 2004 (Taylor 2007).

This episode illustrates a missed opportunity to make the exchange rate reports more relevant. The Great Intervention was by far the most important official action in the international monetary system at the time. Treasury discussed the Japanese operations in its reports for 2003 and the first half of 2004, mentioned that the department supported monetary expansion in Japan, and indicated that the department was engaged in discussions with Japanese officials. Undersecretary Taylor testified on the intervention at least twice (October 1 and October 30, 2003), reiterating the treatment in the Treasury reports.

However, the extent to which the interventions assisted in the Japanese recovery is disputed (e.g., Fatum and Hutchison 2005), and Taylor himself objected to the Ministry of Finance that it intervened too much in March 2004. In an intriguing memoir after he left the Treasury, Taylor discussed the interventions, his response to the Japanese, and deliberations over target ranges with his counterparts in a new "G-3" (Taylor 2007). During 2006, US automobile companies complained that the yen's weakness was a lingering consequence of the interventions, and members of Congress quoted specifically from Taylor's book when making this case at hearings the following year. Taylor served the transparency of exchange rate policy by treating this episode in his book—but congressional oversight and public discourse would have also been improved by more complete analysis of the episode in the exchange rate reports.

Europe's Monetary Union

The creation of Europe's monetary union in January 1999 was the most momentous shift in the structure of the international monetary system in at least a generation. The new currency, the euro, replaced 11 national currencies (now 15), creating a monetary bloc three-quarters the size of the United States by GDP and a potential competitor to the dollar as an international currency. After the Maastricht Treaty was signed, and at the outset of the convergence process, the Treasury Department generally avoided making public comments on the desirability or feasibility of the monetary union, on the reasoning that the creation of the euro was something for the Europeans alone to decide. Privately, senior officials harbored serious doubts about whether Europe would introduce the economic reforms necessary to make the euro a success. When they began to speak on European monetary integration directly in 1997, Treasury officials affirmed that the United States had a strong interest in a prosperous Europe but warned that greater flexibility in the European economy, in particular labor markets, and greater fiscal consolidation would be necessary to make the project successful.[9] Congressional committees held hearings on the ramifications for the United States at which Treasury officials testified (US Senate 1997, US House of Representatives 1998b). But the treatment of this important topic in the exchange rate reports was limited to one and a half pages in February 1997 (pp. 8–9) and three paragraphs in January 1999 (p. 3). The gist of the passages, half of which were purely descriptive, was that the fate of the dollar remained in the hands of US policymakers and that the EMU's "direct economic impact on the United States was likely to be limited."

Fiscal Policy

The Reagan federal budget deficits were the most important cause of the current account deficits of the 1980s. Although the tax cuts and defense spending increases of that era stimulated the economy initially, that stimulus eventually leaked abroad in the form of capital inflows, dollar appreciation, and a (then) record current account deficit—leaving overall GDP only modestly higher, but with higher interest rates and larger external deficits and debt than would have otherwise been the case.

Lawmakers were guided partly by this lesson when drafting the exchange rate provisions of the 1988 Act, which embraced more than just exchange rate policy, but also fundamental underlying macroeconomic policies in both the United States and its economic partners. The provisions stressed the need for greater macroeconomic policy coordination

---

9. See Lawrence H. Summers, speech entitled "EMU: An American View of Europe" at the Euromoney Conference, US Treasury Department press release, April 30, 1997; Timothy F. Geithner, speech entitled "The EMU, the United States, and the World Economy" to a conference of the Konrad Adenauer-Stiftung and Aspen Institute, Washington, May 7, 1998; and Edwin Truman, speech entitled "The Single Currency and Europe's Role in the World Economy" at the World Affairs Council, US Treasury Department press release, Washington, April 6, 1999. US official views are reviewed in Henning (2000, 12–17).

and declared that it was US policy "to achieve macroeconomic policies and exchange rate policies consistent with more appropriate and sustainable balances . . ." (section 3002). The accountability of the president should be increased specifically for "the impact of economic policies and exchange rates on trade competitiveness" (section 3003). The section detailing the contents of the reports (3005) mandated treatment of the factors underlying exchange market conditions and "recommendations for any changes necessary in United States economic policy to attain a more appropriate and sustainable balance in the current account," among other things. The current account balance is by definition a simple function of the overall savings-investment balance; but the budget balance is the element of this equation that is most susceptible to government policy. Therefore, although the specific word "fiscal" does not appear in the reporting requirements section, it is hard to imagine how the section's mandate could be fulfilled without specifically addressing fiscal policy.[10]

The reports' treatment of fiscal policy varies over time from neglectful to substantial, with most reports treating the connection to current account balances fairly superficially. The reports give greater attention to fiscal policy when the budget deficit is decreasing than when it is increasing. Most treatments in the reports take decisions to cut the fiscal deficit as given and examine the consequences for the external balance, rather than analyzing the consequences of fiscal options for the current account in advance as input to decisions on budgets and taxes.

The reports submitted by Secretary Brady under the George H. W. Bush administration treated the connection between fiscal policy and the current account balances cursorily until late 1992. The first report noted the reduction in the federal budget deficit from 6.3 percent to just over 3 percent of GDP from 1983 to 1988 and duly reported the advice of the IMF in the Article IV consultations to reduce the deficit further (US Treasury report, October 1988, 4, 36). The reports that followed noted deficit reduction agreements between the president and Congress and argued that these agreements would contribute to macroeconomic policy coordination in the G-7, the relevant sections of whose communiqués were summarized. Far from declining, however, US budget deficits increased substantially from 1989 to 1993 and were projected to be roughly 5.5 percent of GDP at the close of the Bush administration. Treasury's final report devoted a page and a half to rebutting calls from

---

10. The 1988 Act also required the Office of Management and Budget (OMB), and the budget committees of both houses, to analyze the connection between the budget and the trade balance in their annual budget assessments. See the "Federal Budget Competitiveness Impact Statement," Omnibus Trade and Competitiveness Act of 1988, title V, subtitle D. The OMB provided only cursory analysis, and the provision lapsed after five fiscal years, leaving the exchange rate provisions as the one remaining requirement to address this connection.

IMF staff to reduce the deficit by 5 percent of GDP over the following five years, arguing that this could harm the fragile recovery from the 1991 recession.[11] US current account deficits, which were nearly eliminated in 1991,[12] began to grow thereafter.

The December 1992 report acknowledged that the external deficit would grow—for the first time since the reports were inaugurated—and relayed the IMF argument that fiscal deficits would have "major implications for the health and durability of the economic recovery, domestic investment, and the US current account." In general terms, the report acknowledged that the savings-investment balance affected external balances and that "government dissavings" was part of that equation. But the report stopped shy of explicitly acknowledging that growth in the fiscal deficit would cause the external deficit to be greater than would otherwise be the case. The text instead dances assiduously around that explicit connection.

The first reports by the Clinton administration trumpeted the 1993 agreement with Congress that was projected to reduce the budget deficit by $500 billion cumulatively over the following years, and briefly reported consultations with the IMF on this score (US Treasury reports, May 1993, 12–13; and November 1993, 2, 18.) Indeed, under Secretaries Bentsen, Rubin, and Summers, the federal budget balance shifted from a $255 billion deficit in FY1993 to a $236 billion surplus in FY2000, a change of roughly 6½ percent of GDP. As this shift became apparent, Treasury officials might well have been tempted to forecast a substantial drop in the current account deficit. A couple of these reports made the connection more explicitly, one saying, "Continued progress in reducing the federal budget deficit will also tend to reduce the current account deficit over the medium term by reducing the disparity between levels of aggregate national saving and investment" (US Treasury report, February 1997, 11). A marked decline in private savings, however, ensured that the external deficit grew continuously, with the exception of 1995, throughout the Clinton administration.

The current account deficit for 2000 registered $416 billion.[13] There was already a growing discussion in academic circles and more broadly about how long the growth in external deficits could be sustained (see Mann 1999). Yet, upon taking office, George W. Bush proposed a large package of tax cuts, which, in combination with the slowing of the economy in 2001 and spending decisions, would eliminate the budget surplus and resurrect large budget deficits. One key test of the usefulness of the

---

11. In the event, the deficit was in fact reduced by about that much over this five-year period. See the *Economic Report of the President*, February 1999.

12. Helped by a $42 billion transfer in connection with the "Desert Storm" invasion of Iraq.

13. See the *Economic Report of the President*, February 2007, 400.

exchange rate reports is whether they highlighted the consequences of fiscal policy for external balances. Although the reports discussed the savings-investment arithmetic of the current account in broad terms, however, the specific connection between tax cuts, fiscal deficits, and the current account was virtually ignored during the second Bush's first term.

Once the deterioration in the budget balance was reversed, the reports acknowledged that reducing global imbalances in an orderly manner required "further reducing budget deficits and boosting national saving in the United States . . ." (US Treasury report, November 2005, 1). The reports after November 2005 gave more serious attention to the connection with external balances. As the current account balance continued to deteriorate into 2006, though, the reports warned that the connection was considerably more complex than a reduction in the fiscal deficit translating into a one-for-one reduction in the external deficit (US Treasury reports, November 2005, 6–8; May 2006, 10–15; June 2007, 4, 11–12). These reports stressed the sustained rate of investment in the United States and the attractiveness of US financial assets to international investors as the driver for the current account deficits.

The shift in the budget balance under the Bush administration's first term by nearly 5 percent of GDP—from a surplus of 1.3 percent in FY2001 to a deficit of 3.6 percent in FY2004—was the biggest fiscal expansion since the inauguration of the exchange rate reports. The absence of serious analysis in the reports for 2001–04 thus represents their most critical omission. This failure is especially striking when the broader context is considered. First, as mentioned, the substantive connection was a key lesson of the 1980s, and the external consequences of that decade prompted Congress to establish the reporting requirements. Second, US fiscal policy was being made in a dramatically changed international economic environment. By creating a potential alternative to the dollar, Europe's monetary union had potentially raised the cost to the United States of fiscal choices such as these, costs specifically in terms not only of external deficits but also of the role of the dollar in international financial markets over the long term.[14] If the dollar's role declines during 2008–15,[15] fiscal choices at the beginning of the present decade will likely prove to have been important causes, and the exchange rate reports to date have contributed little to our appreciation of the connection.

To some extent, the reports' neglect during 2001–02 was mirrored by a lack of attention to the external consequences in the broader public discourse over fiscal policy. Few analysts drew this connection in their commentary on fiscal policy at this time—one notable exception being C. Fred

---

14. See, for example, Masson, Krueger, and Turtelboom (1997) and Henning (1997).

15. The future of the international role of the dollar is treated by, among others, Helleiner and Kirshner (2008) and Cohen (2004).

Bergsten.[16] This highlights a key reason for Treasury to address fiscal policy in these reports: the connection and the tradeoffs between fiscal and external policy choices should frame the public debate over policy as well as inform Congress.

The external consequences of the fiscal stance relate directly to foreign borrowing, the appropriate and sustainable limits of which Congress expected Treasury to discuss in the reports (US Congress 1988, 843). Prior to the first Treasury report back in October 1988, the chairmen of the House and Senate banking committees had asked Secretary Brady to specify what would constitute an "appropriate and sustainable" current account balance and "the appropriate goal for . . . the buildup of US net foreign indebtedness." Representative John J. LaFalce (D-NY) wrote Secretary Brady that it was "imperative" that the report specify these and determine whether the prevailing policies were consistent with them.[17] But Treasury has never provided these assessments.

There are, of course, compelling political and bureaucratic reasons why secretaries of the Treasury might wish to avoid drawing attention to the external consequences of fiscal policy decisions. Highlighting the shift toward external deficits produced by budget deficits can undercut political support for, and the political benefit of, tax cuts and spending increases. When key decisions on fiscal programs are set by the president, as they were under George W. Bush, drawing those connections can cause confrontation between Treasury and White House officials. The requirement to address this connection can therefore sometimes place the Treasury between a political rock and hard place.

This, however, was an essential point of the 1988 Act. While one might sympathize with officials who must bring unwelcome analysis to their counterparts in other agencies and the White House, drawing the substantive connection between fiscal policy, the exchange rate, and external balances is essential for good economic governance. The connection is best made by the executive, within which the Treasury is the best place to locate this important task because the secretary is the chief financial officer of the government, has responsibilities over fiscal and exchange rate policies, and represents the United States in the IMF, among other international organizations, and the G-7, where these connections are also often made. Having to acknowledge and manage the tradeoffs is the consequence of having broad responsibility over and leadership in these policy areas.

---

16. See C. Fred Bergsten, "America Cannot Afford Tax Cuts," *Financial Times*, January 11, 2001.

17. See Senator William Proxmire, letter to Secretary Nicholas Brady, October 1988; Representatives Robert Garcia, Fernand J. St. Germain, and John J. LaFalce, letter to Secretary Nicholas Brady, October 14, 1988; Representative John J. LaFalce, letter to Secretary Nicholas Brady, October 13, 1988.

In sum, (1) it is important to have a government document that clearly analyzes the connection between fiscal and external balances and the tradeoffs associated with it; (2) the Treasury Department should prepare and issue that analysis in these reports; and (3) Congress and the watchful public more broadly should ensure that Treasury carries out this important responsibility.

China, 2000–2007

During the Asian financial crisis, China maintained its peg to the dollar, to the relief of most governments in the region as well as the international community. China maintained this policy afterward as well, despite substantial increases in productivity and sustained emerging external surpluses (on both the current and capital accounts). The countries stricken by the crisis were determined not to repeat it and, among other strategies, managed their currencies at stable competitive rates by intervening in the currency markets. As a result, China and its East Asian neighbors began to accumulate large amounts of foreign exchange, mostly US dollars, at the beginning of the present decade. China stood out, however, as the most consistent and largest purchaser of dollars, surpassing Japan in total foreign exchange reserves in 2006.[18]

The case of China consequently riveted public attention on the Treasury reports and spawned legislative proposals in Congress on the reporting process and measures to remedy currency manipulation. The evolution of Treasury's position on Chinese manipulation raises several interesting points. This section reviews the findings of the reports, their analysis of manipulation, conflicts with congressional preferences, and the importance of designation.

Findings

In the "manipulation" section of its reports during 1999 and 2000, Treasury took note of China's peg to the dollar and its rising bilateral trade surplus with the United States. Although a declining overall current account surplus exculpated China from manipulation, the reports reproduced excerpts from a speech by Treasury Secretary Lawrence Summers

---

18. The China case has been treated, and debated, extensively. Critical contributions include Dooley, Folkerts-Landau, and Garber (2003); Eichengreen (2004); Goldstein (2004, 2005); Goldstein and Lardy (2005, 2008); and McKinnon (2006). See also C. Fred Bergsten, statement before the Hearing on US Economic Relations with China: Strategies and Options on Exchange Rates and Market Access, Subcommittee on Security and International Trade and Finance, Committee on Banking, Housing and Urban Affairs, United States Senate, Washington, May 23, 2007.

warning against the type of peg that was common in East Asia prior to the 1997–98 crisis and that China continued to maintain: "[I]t is clear to us that a fixed, but not firmly institutionalized exchange rate regime holds enormous risks for emerging market economies . . ." (US Treasury report, March 2000, 13). The final report of the Treasury under Summers stated that in bilateral discussions, the department had "urged the Chinese authorities to move, over time, to a more flexible exchange rate regime" (US Treasury report, January 2001, 13).

Under Paul O'Neill, the first secretary under the Bush administration, Treasury reports became dramatically shorter in length, the format changed noticeably, and the treatment of potential "manipulators" was folded into the main analysis rather than examined in a separate section. Treasury did not use the report to send signals to China or Congress regarding its attitude toward the renminbi, despite steady increases in China's external surpluses. Under questioning from Senate Banking Committee Chairman Paul Sarbanes (D-MD) during oversight hearings in May 2002, Secretary O'Neill denied that China's exchange rate regime was a serious problem for the United States (US Senate 2002).

The October 2003 report marked an important change. Under the leadership of Secretary John Snow, Treasury officials stated clearly that the renminbi peg "is not appropriate for a major economy like China and should be changed." The document reported that Snow had proposed to Chinese officials that they move to a more "flexible market-based exchange rate regime" (it did not specifically call for appreciation or revaluation) and reduce controls on capital flows (US Treasury report, October 2003, 7).

Subsequent reports ratcheted up the tone of urgency on this topic, as attention from Congress grew with the size of the trade imbalances. Treasury's May 2005 report declared, "If current trends continue without alteration, China's policies will likely meet the statute's technical requirements for designation [for manipulation]. . . . It is now widely accepted that China is now ready and should move without delay in a manner and magnitude that is sufficiently reflective of underlying market conditions" (p. 2). This language was widely interpreted as a threat to cite for manipulation in the subsequent report. This statement and Treasury's discussions with Chinese officials behind the scenes probably contributed to the mid-course correction that followed.

In July 2005, Chinese authorities revalued the renminbi by slightly more than 2 percent and reformed the exchange rate regime (People's Bank of China 2005), abandoning the peg and allowing a gradual upward appreciation. The November 2005 report stated that Treasury refrained from designating China because of its abandonment of the fixed peg and its stated commitment to market-determined currency flexibility. Treasury added that China's commitment to emphasizing domestic sources of growth and financial modernization also contributed to the decision

(p. 2). Since the July 2005 revaluation, the renminbi has appreciated against the dollar by a further 14 percent, but on a nominal effective basis by only a further 6 percent. By this broader measure, the renminbi's value has hardly changed since 2000,[19] and productivity in the tradable goods sector has increased rapidly. Accordingly, China's global current account surplus has continued to soar, reaching 9 percent of GDP in 2006 and probably about 12 percent in 2007. Treasury continued to say that Chinese exchange rate policy was inappropriate, that the Chinese should introduce greater "flexibility,"[20] and that the department discussed these matters with the Chinese authorities extensively. But Treasury waited until its June 2007 report to declare the renminbi "undervalued" (p. 32; see also the December 2007 report, 35)—after the IMF's bilateral surveillance report had announced that conclusion. As of this writing, Treasury has not cited China again for manipulation.

Analysis of Manipulation

The criteria that Treasury enunciates for determining manipulation have been vague and have shifted over time. Although IMF decisions provide some guidance on the meaning of the term, the 1988 Act does not define it, and each team of political appointees to the Treasury department has taken a somewhat different approach. During the early 1990s, Treasury did not enunciate clear criteria that it would use but made clear that it was citing China for its bilateral and global surpluses combined with its close management of the exchange rate through controls and intervention. Although Treasury sustained criticism for citing each of the three countries for manipulation (Korea and Taiwan along with China),[21] its application was a defensible interpretation of the language in the 1988 Act and was not challenged by the banking committees. The December 1995 report (pp. 11–13) contained four criteria—external balances, exchange restrictions and capital controls, exchange rate movements, and movements in reserves—which were expanded to five with the addition of macroeconomic trends in February 1997. Because it was on the new criterion that China, whose growth was slowing, was exonerated in January 1999, an independent outside observer should be forgiven for expecting that, when Chinese economic growth accelerated, the Treasury would cite China if the other criteria remained satisfied. But the O'Neill Treasury

---

19. Using the JPMorgan nominal effective exchange rate index.

20. The term "flexibility" could be construed to include a one-shot revaluation and an upward managed float, of course, but is ultimately ambiguous with respect to the expected direction of movement.

21. See Lardy (1994). See also statements by C. Fred Bergsten and John Williamson before the US Senate hearing in 1989, as detailed in footnote 1 of this chapter.

reduced the criteria to two—exchange restrictions and exchange rate movements—qualifying the latter by saying that real equilibrium exchange rates are "difficult to define" (US Treasury report, October 2001, 10).[22] The Snow Treasury expanded the number of criteria to seven—exchange rates, external balances, reserves, macroeconomic trends, monetary and financial developments, state of institutional development, and financial and exchange restrictions—but did not elaborate on them as had the Rubin/Summers reports.

By 2004, members of Congress had become concerned enough about Treasury's reluctance to find manipulation that they took two actions. First, they attached to the department's FY2005 appropriation a requirement for a separate report on the criteria used to make the manipulation determination. Second, they initiated a study of these reports by the Government Accountability Office (GAO). Thus in March 2005, Treasury delivered to the appropriations committees a substantial, in-depth paper on the criteria it used to determine manipulation (US Treasury 2005). The GAO, which released its report in April, noted that the factors in Treasury's reports varied over time and that the weights attached to them by the department when assessing manipulation were not transparent. But the GAO complimented the March 2005 Treasury paper as a "high-level discussion" (GAO 2005).

Treasury responded in its November 2005 exchange rate report by attaching an appendix entitled "Analysis of Exchange Rates Pursuant to the Act." The appendix presented six specific measures, subjected to three weighting schemes, and evaluated 23 trading partners. These indicators—trade and current account balances, protracted large-scale intervention in one direction, rapid foreign exchange reserve accumulation, capital controls and payments restrictions, measures of undervaluation and real effective exchange rate movements, and unusually heavy reliance on net exports for growth—echo some of the criteria for identifying manipulation in the IMF guidelines for exchange rate surveillance. Given the absence of guidance on the interpretation of this term in the 1988 Act, and the fact that the act's language was borrowed from Article IV, these guidelines are certainly relevant.[23] But Treasury also adopted the interpretation of the guidelines that stressed intent and gave deference to the declaration of purpose of the target of the investigation. Thus, in the June 2007 report, after reviewing the data and concluding that the renminbi was undervalued, Treasury stated that it did not cite China for manipulation because it was "unable to determine that China's exchange rate policy was

---

22. Treasury later argued, however, that determining undervaluation was distinct from determining manipulation and that the 1988 Act did not require the former (GAO 2005).

23. The reports do not refer explicitly to the IMF's guidelines on exchange rate policy, but such a reference is contained in the March 2005 report to the appropriations committees.

carried out for the purpose of preventing effective balance of payments adjustment or gaining unfair competitive advantage in international trade" (p. 2). Note, however, that the question of intent had not barred Treasury from citing China, Korea, and Taiwan during 1988–94.

Since early 2005, Treasury officials have mounted a good faith effort to give greater analytical content to the concept of manipulation and to improve the exchange rate reports generally. The reports have become somewhat more detailed and incisive, and Treasury has produced occasional papers reviewing models of equilibrium exchange rates and international economic policy coordination (McCowan, Pollard, and Weeks 2007; Sobel and Stedman 2006). For these efforts, Treasury is to be complimented.[24] But Treasury waited until opposition to Chinese exchange rate policy built up a substantial head of steam on Capitol Hill. In March 2005, Senator Charles Schumer (D-NY) offered an amendment, on a procedural motion, to impose 27.5 percent tariffs on imports from China. The amendment received 67 votes, and since then Treasury has been on the defensive on this issue.

The Treasury papers are correct that analysis of equilibrium exchange rates is complicated, and different models produce different estimates. However, model uncertainty need not prevent a finding of manipulation. When a country intervenes massively in one direction over several years while running ever-larger external surpluses and accumulating unprecedented quantities of foreign reserves, a sophisticated model is not needed to know that its currency is below the equilibrium value and frustrating balance of payments adjustment. In China's case, model uncertainty would be a transparent excuse for failure to designate for manipulation, and in fact Treasury's reports during 2006 and 2007 affirm the need for a change in China's regime. The department's rationale for not designating the country for manipulation now rests entirely on the "intent defense."

Treasury has nonetheless pursued the bilateral negotiations that it would have been required to pursue under the 1988 law if it had cited China for manipulation. Beginning under Secretary O'Neill, but especially under Secretary Snow, Treasury conducted serious talks with the Chinese Ministry of Finance and the People's Bank of China, among other Chinese actors. Treasury Secretary Henry Paulson launched the Strategic Economic Dialogue, in which exchange rates figure prominently and which engages several US cabinet secretaries and the Federal Reserve chairman with Chinese ministers under the leadership of a deputy premier. Treasury clearly recognizes that the exchange rate is a critical issue, as does the administration more broadly, and is willing to press Chinese

---

24. For a review of Treasury's efforts in this regard, see Mark Sobel, statement before the Joint Hearing on Currency Manipulation and Its Effects on US Business and Workers, Ways and Means Committee, Committee on Energy and Commerce, and Committee on Financial Services, United States House of Representatives, Washington, May 9, 2007.

counterparts, even if not as forcefully as many members of Congress and independent analysts would prefer.

The underlying explanation for President Bush's successive Treasury secretaries' refusal to cite China for manipulation appears to be threefold. First, the department and the US government more broadly have a number of other economic and foreign policy "fish to fry" with China, and securing renminbi revaluation, while important, is not a top government priority. Second, administration officials believe that citing China would be tactically counterproductive, making their Beijing counterparts more rather than less reluctant to revalue. Third, as of 2007, international support for the US position has been insufficient. The unwillingness of the IMF to pursue special consultations and cite China for manipulation was problematic for a US designation. Senior Treasury officials agree with the basic diagnosis that the Chinese currency is undervalued and should be revalued, and have pursued this objective in bilateral negotiations. It would be reasonable to conclude that, in this context, Treasury officials believe that it would be a mistake on political grounds, irrespective of the economic and legal merits, to designate China for manipulation. Treasury officials might also fear that citing China for manipulation would reduce their freedom of maneuver on the matter, incite members of Congress to invoke punitive measures if negotiations were not more fruitful, and increase pressure to cite other countries as well.[25]

Manipulation and Accountability

Morris Goldstein (2006), Goldstein and Lardy (2005, 2008), and Michael Mussa (2007), along with C. Fred Bergsten,[26] are among those who have made a compelling case that China has manipulated its exchange rate within the meaning of the IMF's Article IV (see appendix B in this book). Mussa (2007) forcefully advances an assertive interpretation, arguing that the injunction against manipulation should be read in the context of the purposes of the IMF, which are, inter alia, to facilitate "balanced growth of international trade," "avoid competitive exchange depreciation," and reduce "disequilibrium" in payments balances (Article I (ii), (iii), and

---

25. On the other hand, renminbi hawks argue that citing China for manipulation could also garner greater credibility in Congress, increase bargaining leverage with Chinese authorities, and discourage other Asian countries from following the Chinese approach.

26. C. Fred Bergsten, statement before the Hearing on US Economic Relations with China: Strategies and Options on Exchange Rates and Market Access, Subcommittee on Security and International Trade and Finance, Committee on Banking, Housing and Urban Affairs, United States Senate, Washington, May 23, 2007.

27. The position of the IMF's General Counsel on the interpretation of these articles is presented in IMF (2006) and the members' response to the weaknesses in exchange rate surveillance in IMF (2007).

(vi)).[27] He concludes that the Fund's surveillance of China's exchange rate policy "constitutes gross misfeasance, malfeasance, and nonfeasance."

A reasonable reading of the exchange rate provisions of the 1988 Act also generates a critical judgment of Treasury's nondesignation of China for manipulation. That reading must ultimately be guided by US law, legislative history, and congressional intent, rather than the IMF articles—although countries' IMF obligations might help to inform our understanding of congressional intent. The statute itself offers little guidance as to the meaning of the term "manipulation" or the relevance of intent in finding it. But the Congress clearly expected that the Asian NIEs that had restrained appreciation of their currencies during the mid-1980s would be cited for manipulation by Treasury, as indeed South Korea, Taiwan, and eventually China were (US Congress 1988, 841–42). Given that Chinese policy behavior during 2000–2007 was more extreme and more consequential than the NIE policies of the late 1980s, one can conclude that congressional intent would call for a designation in this case as well.

It is worth emphasizing that the problem of divining intent to prevent payments adjustment on the part of foreign authorities did not prevent Treasury from citing China, Korea, and Taiwan for manipulation during 1988–94. Treasury has not explained why determining intent was possible then but was not possible in 2007.[28] Moreover, the 1988 Act does not provide a waiver from the manipulation designation in cases where that designation could be tactically counterproductive or politically inconvenient; instead Treasury can waive the requirement to initiate negotiations once the designation is made. So, it is difficult to reconcile the refusal of President Bush's Treasury secretaries to cite China for manipulation with the letter and spirit of the 1988 Act—which raises the question of their accountability to the Congress in this important respect.

Importance of Designation

Some commentators might argue that as long as Treasury pursues the negotiations that were mandated by the 1988 Act, it makes little difference whether the secretary formally designates China as a manipulator. However, four considerations suggest the contrary—that using the "m word," when justified, has important consequences and is more likely than temporizing to produce policy change on the part of offenders.

First, the designation is important from the standpoint of process and accountability. The 1988 Act lays down a specific procedure: the Treasury Department is to assess, designate, initiate, or waive negotiations, and, if negotiations proceed, report on them. In the Strategic Economic Dialogue

---

28. GAO (2005, 13–16) discusses Treasury's rationales for its manipulation decisions regarding China but sheds little light on the problem of intent.

with China, for example, the Treasury addresses the exchange rate issue along with a number of other negotiating objectives, and tradeoffs are inevitably made among them. But the law does not provide for using the manipulation issue as leverage for concessions on other issues (such as access to the Chinese market for US financial institutions); the negotiations are to ensure that manipulators "adjust the rate of exchange" to "permit effective balance of payments adjustments and to eliminate the unfair advantage." By moving to negotiations without designating China for manipulation, Treasury is not restricted to this objective and is not required to report on the negotiations or on the tradeoffs that they might involve. Treasury consults with members of Congress on the Strategic Economic Dialogue with China, but that consultation is voluntary, informal, and not transparent. It releases statements on the results of the dialogue,[29] but their release and content are voluntary. So, negotiating without designating redirects bargaining in ways the law might not intend and potentially weakens oversight.

Second, designating for manipulation would signal to the US public that the Treasury is serious about combating the practice. In the United States, as elsewhere, broad political support for economic openness depends in part on the perception that foreign governments are not intervening in the marketplace on behalf of their producers at the expense of American firms and workers. When investment, trade, wages, and employment in particular sectors or regions are affected by the intervention of foreign governments, confidence that globalization will operate with fairness wanes. Using plain language to describe a widely known practice—calling a spade a spade—gives greater confidence to interest groups and the public at large that the US government recognizes the problem, takes it seriously, and is moving to solve it.

Third, designating for manipulation would signal to the international community that the Treasury is not only serious about combating manipulation but also expects others to cooperate. Designating a country such as China would probably entail a backlash, which both international organizations and national governments would prefer to avoid. As an international organization that depends on the political support of its members, the IMF shies away from designating China for manipulation. By taking the lead and designating, the US Treasury would encourage and reinforce the IMF in its enhancement of exchange rate surveillance. Conversely, the US government cannot expect the IMF to challenge important members on their currency practices unless the US Treasury is willing to do so as well.

Finally, designation for manipulation could strengthen the Treasury's bargaining position with manipulators and improve prospects for

---

29. The statements are available on Treasury's US–China Strategic Economic Dialogue website at www.treas.gov/initiatives/us-china (accessed March 19, 2008).

remediation. Treasury officials have argued that the opposite is more likely to be the case, that the Chinese government would halt negotiations. Chinese officials would undoubtedly be offended. But the accomplishments of the Strategic Economic Dialogue to date are questionable and the Chinese current account surplus has continued to rise. So Treasury's tactics do not appear to have been particularly fruitful, and a new approach is warranted. Beijing has demonstrated pragmatism on a number of other economic matters, such as trade cases before the WTO. Moreover, designation proved to be a negotiating asset rather than a liability during the manipulation cases of the late 1980s and early 1990s.

Assessment

So, we return to the questions posed at the outset: How well has the accountability process worked? Do the Treasury's exchange rate reports present new information in a timely manner that Congress cares about and that allows the committees of jurisdiction to assess whether Treasury is meeting the objectives set for it under the 1988 Act and other legislation? This section considers the answers to these questions and briefly compares the exchange rate reports with the Federal Reserve's reports on monetary policy.

Overall Evaluation

The Treasury's approach to the reporting process has varied from one administration to the next. The George H. W. Bush administration integrated the reports into its strategy vis-à-vis both the G-7 countries and the NIEs. These early reports were longer and treated international coordination in more detail than subsequent ones. These reports and the reasonably diligent follow-up by the congressional committees make this initial period the "high point" of the accountability process. The Clinton administration, while improving the reports that it submitted over time, treated them as a sideshow to the crises in Mexico and Asia, which it addressed through different channels to the Congress. The first administration of Clinton's successor, George W. Bush, treated the reports as a pro forma exercise, drastically shrank them in size, and virtually ignored the consequences of the Bush tax cuts for the external balance. The reports of 2001–02 and the absence of follow-up on the House side make this period the "low point" of the accountability process.

Under Bush's second term, congressional scrutiny forced the administration to take the reports more seriously. The quality of the reports has improved substantially since 2005, with more attention to the relationship between fiscal policy and the current account and the potential risks of growing external indebtedness. Recent reports also contain appendices—on sovereign wealth funds and reserve adequacy, for example—that congressional staff have found useful. The most recent reports are critical of Chinese policy and recommend specific changes, including currency appreciation. Former Undersecretary Timothy Adams and officials in Treasury's Office of International Affairs deserve substantial credit for these improvements. Unfortunately, the secretary's refusal to designate China for manipulation—the main focus of political attention—overshadowed these constructive steps, and these improvements could be reversed by a future administration.

The 2005 GAO report concluded that Treasury had "generally complied" with the reporting requirements of the 1988 Act. It complained that the reports' discussion of the impact of exchange rates on the US economy had become less specific over time, but took some comfort from Treasury's assurance that it took these effects into consideration (GAO 2005, 16–19). But the scope of the GAO analysis was limited to the narrow standard of whether Treasury satisfied the strict requirements of the law. When one asks whether the reports provide a firm foundation for oversight and address policy questions of contemporary interest—more comprehensive standards—the conclusion is less favorable.

For much of the period since 1988, then, the reports have been disappointing. They have often been submitted quite late and in some cases not at all, avoided a number of policy questions that were the focus of contemporary attention and political interest, and were backward-looking and more descriptive than analytical. Too often, the reports have appeared to be drafted to satisfy the literal requirement of the law rather than to enunciate, explain, and advance Treasury's policy. While manipulation was found in some circumstances, Treasury failed to find it in one blatant and systemically important case that calls into question the secretary's accountability to the Congress under the 1988 Act.

Responsibility for the quality of the reports lies primarily with the senior political appointees at the Treasury, beginning with the secretary. It is they who make the basic decisions about how the legislative mandate for the reports is addressed, the level of analysis provided, the amount of detail about G-7 discussions, and whether countries will be cited for manipulation, among other basic parameters. On highly political questions, such as major fiscal programs and Chinese currency matters, the secretary might receive guidance from the Office of the President. The capable Treasury staff must work within these guidelines when preparing the reports.

Treasury officials have a natural and understandable desire to keep their exchange rate policy cards close to their vest, preferring to not telegraph their intentions to the markets and to maintain maximum room for maneuver in international negotiations. It might not be in the interest of the country or Congress to require Treasury to give advance notice of or commitment to, for example, exchange market intervention. Nonetheless, there is a middle ground between repackaging information that is already widely known and giving advance warning of policy changes or operations. Without tipping its hand tactically, Treasury could provide more useful and novel analysis, suggestions for which are presented in the concluding chapter.

Comparison with Monetary Policy Reports

Owing to the substantive linkage to monetary policy, and because the reports of the Federal Reserve Board were in the minds of legislators when they wrote the 1988 Act, Treasury's approach to the exchange rate reports merits comparison with the Federal Reserve's approach to its reports originally established by the Full Employment and Balanced Growth Act of 1978, commonly known as the Humphrey-Hawkins Act. First, the monetary policy reports are mildly informative about the future forecast for inflation and thinking in the Federal Open Market Committee (FOMC).[30] Additional documents, including the minutes of FOMC meetings, the *Federal Reserve Bulletin*, and statistics, supplement these reports. Collectively, these reports are considerably more informative about monetary policy and the Federal Reserve's approach to it than the Treasury's reports are about its approach to exchange rate policy. Second, although the Federal Reserve has a dual mandate to pursue "maximum employment" and "stable prices," it has a good record of meeting its statutory objectives, whereas Treasury's position on Chinese currency manipulation is arguably at odds with congressional intent. Third, and importantly, the Federal Reserve consistently delivers its reports on time, in stark contrast to Treasury's practice. The Federal Reserve has not delayed submissions even on the threshold of important international meetings or in the face of market instability—reasons the Treasury has sometimes used to delay submission of the exchange rate report.[31]

Notably, both the Federal Reserve and the Treasury department resisted their respective reporting requirements when first imposed by the Congress. But the Federal Reserve gradually warmed to them as a useful instrument for communicating its policies and intentions. Chairman Ben S. Bernanke's July 2007 testimony was almost effusive: "In establishing these hearings [30 years ago], the Congress proved prescient in anticipating the

---

30. See, for example, Board of Governors of the Federal Reserve System, *Monetary Policy Report to the Congress*, July 18, 2007, 1–4, available at www.federalreserve.gov (accessed March 19, 2008).

31. Reviews of the monetary policy reports and relations between Congress and the Federal Reserve include Woolley (1984), Havrilesky (1995), US House of Representatives (1995), and Morris (2000).

worldwide trend toward greater transparency and accountability. . . . Over the years, these testimonies and the associated reports have proved an invaluable vehicle for the Federal Reserve's communication with the public about monetary policy. . . ."[32] By contrast, although Secretary Brady and Undersecretary Mulford made similar comments about the exchange rate reports and hearings in 1989, any enthusiasm for the reporting requirement by Treasury officials since then has been difficult to detect.

There are, admittedly, several differences between monetary and exchange rate policy that might explain some of the differences in the two agencies' approach to their reporting obligations. The Federal Reserve is independent, whereas the Treasury is political. The Federal Reserve's report is primarily domestic, whereas Treasury's report involves relationships with foreign governments. Conventional wisdom has evolved to favor transparency in monetary policy, but not nearly so much in the realm of exchange rate policy. This comparison nonetheless suggests that there is considerable room for Treasury to embrace the reports as part of a modern communications strategy and to welcome its accountability to the Congress.

32. Ben S. Bernanke, statement before the Hearing on Semiannual Monetary Policy Report to the Congress, Committee on Banking, Housing and Urban Affairs, United States Senate, July 19, 2007.

Appendix 4A

Table 4A.1 Overview of the US Treasury's reports on international economic and exchange rate policy, 1988–2007

Report number	Date due	Date submitted	Notable topics treated[a]	Countries reviewed for manipulation	Countries cited for manipulation	Committee and date of congressional hearings
1	October 15, 1988	October 24, 1988	■ International economic policy coordination; G-7 commitment to exchange rate stability ■ US current account and trade deficits; fiscal adjustment ■ Asian newly industrialized economies' (NIEs) current account surpluses ■ Structural reforms in developing countries	Korea, Taiwan, Hong Kong, Singapore	Korea, Taiwan	None
2	April 15, 1989	April 1989	■ Slower pace of external adjustments ■ US fiscal adjustment ■ G-7 exchange market cooperation and intervention	Korea, Taiwan	Korea, Taiwan	Senate Banking, 101st Congress, 1st Session, May 5
3	October 15, 1989	October 27, 1989	■ Inflationary pressures (Japan, Germany) ■ US budget and current account deficit ■ Bilateral exchange rate negotiations with Asian NIEs on financial policies and capital market restrictions	Korea, Taiwan	Korea	Senate Banking, Subcommittee on International Finance and Monetary Policy, November 16; House Banking, Subcommittee on Development, Finance, Trade and Monetary Policy, 101st Congress, 1st Session, October 31
4	April 15, 1990	April 18, 1990	■ Reduction in global external imbalances ■ Reforms in Eastern Europe ■ Depreciation of yen ■ Asian NIEs' current account surpluses	Taiwan, Korea	None	Senate Banking, April 19; House Banking, 101st Congress, 2nd Session, May 9

#						
5	October 15, 1990	December 3, 1990	• The Gulf crisis, oil price, inflationary pressures, and twin risks • Exchange market coordination • Unification of Germany • US fiscal adjustment • Economic and exchange rate development in Asian NIEs	Korea, Taiwan, China	None	None
6	April 15, 1991	May 1991	• Slower global growth; US and UK recessions • Reduction in current account imbalances • Call for G-7 actions to reduce real interest rates • Economic and exchange rate development in NIEs	Korea, Taiwan, China	None	Senate Banking, 102nd Congress, 1st Session, May 16
7	October 15, 1991	November 1991	• External imbalances (especially Japan) • Interest rates (especially Germany) • Economic reform in Eastern Europe, Latin America • Uruguay Round • Asian NIE current account surpluses	Korea, Taiwan, China	None	Senate Banking, Subcommittee on International Finance and Monetary Policy, 102nd Congress, 1st Session, November 12
8	April 15, 1992	May 12, 1992	• Decrease in inflation and strong growth • G-7 fiscal deficits • High real interest rates (especially Germany) • Asian NIE current account surpluses, economic and exchange rate developments	Korea, Taiwan, China	Taiwan, China	Senate Banking, Subcommittee on International Finance and Monetary Policy, 102nd Congress, 2nd Session, May 12
9	October 15, 1992	December 1992	• Global expansion • Japan's fiscal stimulus • Need for better understanding of global capital markets • Bilateral exchange rate negotiations with Asian NIEs	Korea, Taiwan, China	Taiwan, China	None

Note: The full texts of the reports between August 1996 and November 2005 are available on the US Treasury website at www.treas.gov/press/archives. The most recent reports are available at www.treas.gov/offices/international-affairs/economic-exchange-rates.

(table continues next page)

Table 4A.1   Overview of the US Treasury's reports on international economic and exchange rate policy, 1988–2007 *(continued)*

Report number	Date due	Date submitted	Notable topics treated[a]	Countries reviewed for manipulation	Countries cited for manipulation	Committee and date of congressional hearings
10	April 15, 1993	May 23, 1993	• Weak growth in Japan and Europe • Need to intensify international policy coordination • US fiscal deficit; Japan's current account surplus • Further trade liberalization • Exchange rate volatility	Korea, Taiwan, China	China	Senate Banking, 103rd Congress, 1st Session, May 23
11	October 15, 1993	November 23, 1993	• US exports • Low growth in Japan and (continental) Europe • Employment • US fiscal adjustment (especially health care) • Yen appreciation and Economic and Monetary Union (EMU)	Korea, Taiwan, China	China	None
12	April 15, 1994	July 21, 1994	• Low inflation but high unemployment • Expansion through adequate policy mix • Depreciation of dollar against yen and deutsche mark • Capital controls in Asian NIEs	Korea, Taiwan, China	China	Senate Banking, 103rd Congress, 2nd Session, July 21
13	October 15, 1994	January 3, 1995	• Global recovery • US current account and budget deficit • Strong dollar policy • Capital controls in Asian NIEs • Manipulation	Korea, Taiwan, China	None	None

14	April 15, 1995	August 25, 1995	• Low growth in Japan • Exchange rate volatility and depreciation of dollar • US current account deficit • Mexico crisis • Capital controls in Asian NIEs • Liberalization in China	Korea, Taiwan, China	None	None
15	October 15, 1995	December 15, 1995	• Depreciation of dollar • Exchange rate volatility • US fiscal deficit • Capital controls • Inflation in Asian NIEs	Korea, Taiwan, China	None	None
16	April 15, 1996	August 9, 1996	• G-7 recovery • Appreciation of dollar • Growth in Latin America • Exchange restrictions and capital controls in Asian NIEs	Taiwan, China, Singapore	None	None/extensive follow-up elsewhere
17	October 15, 1996	February 21, 1997	• Exchange rate stability • Moderate global growth • Reduction of Japan's current account surplus	Taiwan, China, Singapore	None	None
18	April 15, 1997	Not issued			
19	October 15, 1997	Not issued			
20	April 15, 1998	Not issued			
21	October 15, 1998	January 22, 1999[b]	• Asian financial crisis • US current account deficit • Appreciation of dollar • Move to floating rates in Asia	Taiwan, China, Singapore, Malaysia	None	None/extensive follow-up elsewhere

(table continues next page)

Table 4A.1   Overview of the US Treasury's reports on international economic and exchange rate policy, 1988–2007 (*continued*)

Report number	Date due	Date submitted	Notable topics treated[a]	Countries reviewed for manipulation	Countries cited for manipulation	Committee and date of congressional hearings
22	April 15, 1999	September 3, 1999[c]	• Economic weakness in emerging markets, Europe, and Japan • Strong net capital inflow in the United States • US current account deficit • Repeats secretary's "strong dollar" language	Korea, Taiwan, China, Singapore, Malaysia	None	None
23	October 15, 1999	Joined with a subsequent report				
24	April 15, 2000	March 9, 2000[d]	• US current account deficit • Strong net capital inflow in the United States • Structural and financial sector reforms in Japan	Korea, Taiwan, China, Malaysia	None	None
25	October 15, 2000	January 18, 2001	• Strong growth in the United States • Higher oil prices and acceleration of US imports • Structural and financial-sector reforms in Japan	Korea, Taiwan, China, Malaysia	None	None
26	April 15, 2001	June 22, 2001	• Slowed US and global growth • Strong net capital inflow in the United States • Money laundering	Korea, Taiwan, China, Malaysia, Russia	None	None

27	October 15, 2001	October 24, 2001	• Slow US and global growth • Depreciation in capital flows to and from the United States • Money laundering and terrorist financing	Korea, Taiwan, China, Malaysia, Russia	None	None
28	April 15, 2002	April 24, 2002	• 9/11 attacks • Export and import contraction in G-7 • Strong net capital inflow in the United States	None	None	Senate Banking, 107th Congress, 2nd Session, May 1
29	October 15, 2002	November 12, 2002	• Continued trend toward exchange rate flexibility • US current account deficit	None	None	None
30	April 15, 2003	May 6, 2003	• US current account deficit • Depreciations in Latin America	None	None	None
31	October 15, 2003	October 30, 2003	• Agenda for growth • High oil prices • China's surplus	China, Japan[e]	None	Senate Banking, 108th Congress, 1st Session, October 30
32	April 15, 2004	April 15, 2004	• US current account and capital account • Japan's recovery • China's exchange rate regime	China, Japan	None	None
33	October 15, 2004	December 3, 2004	• US current account and capital account • Rising interest rates and oil prices • Japan's exchange rate interventions • China's exchange rate regime	China, Japan	None	None
34	April 15, 2005	May 17, 2005	• External adjustments • Greater exchange rate flexibility (especially Asia) • China's exchange rate regime • China's internal reforms	China, Malaysia	None	Senate Banking, 109th Congress, 1st Session, May 26

(table continues next page)

Table 4A.1 Overview of the US Treasury's reports on international economic and exchange rate policy, 1988–2007 *(continued)*

Report number	Date due	Date submitted	Notable topics treated[a]	Countries reviewed for manipulation	Countries cited for manipulation	Committee and date of congressional hearings
35	October 15, 2005	November 27, 2005	• US fiscal deficit and low saving rate • Demand-led growth in Japan and Europe • Greater exchange rate flexibility in Asia • Doha Round • China's exchange rate regime • IMF to promote exchange rate flexibility • Appendix on indicators used for analysis of exchange rates	China, Malaysia	None	None
36	April 15, 2006	May 10, 2006	• Rising oil prices • China's exchange rate policy • Multilateral approach to reforming China's exchange rate regime • Appendices on (1) manipulation indicators; (2) fixed versus flexible exchange rates; (3) China's measures toward renminbi flexibility	China, Malaysia	None	Senate Banking, 109th Congress, 2nd Session, May 18
37	October 15, 2006	December 19, 2006	• Global imbalances • Slow growth in Japan and Europe • Oil prices and oil exporters' economic policies • US fiscal deficit • China's domestic demand, capital account liberalization, and exchange rate regime • Appendices on (1) manipulation indicators; (2) methods for assessing misalignment; (3) adequacy of foreign exchange reserves	China	None	Senate Banking, 110th Congress, 1st Session, January 31

38	April 15, 2007	June 13, 2007	▪ Global imbalances ▪ Strong growth in the United States, Europe, Japan ▪ Oil exporters' economic policies ▪ China's domestic demand, capital account liberalization, and exchange rate regime ▪ Appendices on (1) manipulation indicators; (2) China's trade data; (3) sovereign wealth funds	China	None	None
39	October 15, 2007	December 19, 2007	▪ Housing slump and subprime mortgage crisis ▪ Reduction in US current account deficit, and rapid growth of emerging markets ▪ Depreciation of the dollar ▪ Importance of implementing the June 2007 IMF decision on exchange rate policy surveillance ▪ Need for rebalancing of Chinese economy ▪ "Substantial undervaluation" of the renminbi ▪ Appendices on (1) capital flows and foreign exchange markets; (2) sovereign wealth funds	China	None	None

a. The reports generally treat the subjects of (1) World Economic Performance and Prospects, subdivided into separate treatments of industrial countries and emerging markets, (2) Exchange Market Developments, including foreign exchange market intervention when applicable, (3) US Economy and Balance of Payments, (4) International Coordination, (5) Currency Manipulation, and (6) a statistical appendix—although the emphasis and organization of these treatments vary considerably among reports. This column lists the treatments within these substantive headings that were especially noteworthy or exceptional in light of contemporary economic developments.

b. Period covered: November 1, 1996 to October 31, 1998.

c. Period covered: November 1, 1998 to June 30, 1999.

d. Period covered: July 1, 1999 to December 31, 1999.

e. Report indicated that Treasury was "actively engaged" in discussions with these countries' monetary authorities over their exchange rate policy and intervention practices—the criteria on which these countries and Malaysia are listed as reviewed for manipulation in later reports as well.

5

Congressional Oversight

To underscore the role of Congress in oversight and to bolster Treasury's incentive to take its reports seriously, the Exchange Rates and International Economic Policy Coordination Act of 1988 established that "the Secretary shall appear, if requested, before both committees to provide testimony on these reports." The record of congressional follow-up is summarized in appendix table 5A.1. The banking committees have been more interested in holding hearings on the reports in some periods than in others. From 1988 to 1994, the committees convened 13 hearings, but from 1995 to 2001, the committees held no hearings specifically on the reports. Between January 2002 and June 2007, 11 follow-up hearings were held, nine by the banking committees and two by the House Ways and Means Committee. Thus, congressional committees or their subcommittees have held a combined total of 24 sets of hearings on 26 days since 1988. When the exchange rate issue was salient, committees sometimes held more than one hearing on the same report. Of the 35 reports Treasury submitted, committees held hearings on 15 of them, less than half, with the Senate Banking Committee far more active than its House counterpart.

Congressional oversight on international monetary and financial policies has been broader than simply follow-up on the Treasury reports per se. Committees also held hearings on particular issues, crises, and international organizations that were related to but went beyond the focus of the exchange rate reports. At least 22 hearings were held on the financial crises in Mexico, Asia, Russia, and Argentina. Committees also have held several additional hearings on Chinese exchange rate policy. More broadly still, Congress held at least 73 hearings during 1989–2007 that addressed currency and exchange rate matters in significant measure as part of oversight focusing mainly on international trade, international economics, and international relations. Oversight on these related matters diverted time and energy from the exchange rate reports in both the Treasury and the Congress and accounts in part for the absence of direct follow-up on the reports during 1995–2001.

Party control of the chamber also helps to explain the hiatus in follow-up hearings during 1995–2001. Under Democratic control, Senators William Proxmire (D-WI) and Donald Riegle (D-MI) chaired the Senate Banking Committee during the early years of these reports. Republican Senators Alfonse D'Amato (R-NY) and then Phil Gramm (R-TX) succeeded them as chairmen of the banking committee in the 104th, 105th, and 106th Congresses. On the House side, Representatives Fernand St. Germain (D-RI) and Henry Gonzalez (D-TX) chaired the banking committee under Democratic control. They were replaced by Republican Representative James Leach (R-IA) in 1995 and then Representative Michael Oxley (R-OH) in 2001. The Republican chairmen in both chambers showed little interest in follow-up hearings on the exchange rate reports. Senator Paul Sarbanes (D-MD) resumed the hearings before the Senate Banking Committee when he assumed the chairmanship in the 107th Congress (2001), but the House Committee on Financial Services, as it was renamed, remained in Republican control and conducted comparatively little follow-up on the reports.

The substantive focus of these hearings evolved accordingly. During the early years, members of Congress questioned Treasury officials closely on their findings of manipulation. Their discussions sometimes appeared to be choreographed "good cop, bad cop" routines, wherein the committee members would press Treasury to in turn press the newly industrialized economies for appreciation in the expectation that the Asian press would duly report these encounters in the target countries. During the early period, Treasury officials supported the reporting and oversight process. Secretary Nicholas F. Brady and Undersecretary David C. Mulford praised the reporting process. But their successors were (considerably) less supportive. By the late 1990s, the tardiness of the report became a source of friction when Senator Sarbanes rebuked the Treasury sternly for failure to meet the statutory deadlines (US Senate 1999, 22–23).

During 2002–07, China and its exchange rate regime dominated the hearings. Members repeatedly sought explanations as to why Treasury refused to cite the country for manipulation, prodded officials for the criteria they used when deciding, and were largely unsatisfied with the responses (see the section on China in chapter 4). Thomas Mann and Norman Ornstein (2006) have prominently criticized the Republican Congress for failing to exercise oversight of the executive branch during the two terms of President George W. Bush. But on the issue of Chinese exchange rate policy, Republican and Democratic Congresses have scrutinized administration policy. Congress has been particularly active over the last two years.

Underscoring the concern across committee jurisdictions, the international subcommittees of the House Ways and Means, Financial Services, and Energy and Commerce Committees held a joint hearing on currency manipulation in May 2007. Multicommittee oversight can help draw linkages between trade, exchange rates, and macroeconomic policy (Destler and Henning 1989, 155–57). It is also worth noting that members and committees have exercised oversight in ways other than hearings, such as through letters and conversations between the chairmen and other members, as well as with the secretary and other Treasury officials.[1] Although it is more difficult to evaluate, nonhearing oversight can be important.

Frustrated by Treasury, Congress turned to tactics that had proved fruitful during the standoff with the Reagan administration in the mid-1980s. The hearings helped to raise public awareness and a case for action on currency manipulation. Congress used the budget process and the GAO to extract more clarity from Treasury regarding its stance on China. Furthermore, members pressed beyond reporting requirements and manipulation provisions of the 1988 Act by proposing bills to (1) restrict Treasury's discretion in these circumstances, clarify the concept of manipulation, or transfer these tasks to another agency; and (2) introduce trade measures to compensate for the undervaluation of the renminbi. Appendix table 5A.2 presents an overview of the bills submitted to the 110th Congress.[2] Both of these types of proposals have ratcheted up the pressure on the Paulson Treasury to drive a harder bargain with its Chinese counterparts.

Did Congress play its role in the accountability process effectively? Did it follow up promptly, ask the right questions, and deliver consequences in the instances when Treasury did not report promptly or substantively? When trade issues were prominent, particularly involving countries that manipulated their currencies, members of Congress were fairly diligent in their oversight of Treasury on exchange rates; when trade issues have not been prominent, members have largely neglected the reports. Democrats followed up more diligently than their Republican colleagues as chairmen. Members of Congress have typically been

1. See, for example, the February 9, 2007 letter from House committee chairmen (Representatives Rangel, Levin, Dingell, and Frank) to Secretary Henry Paulson urging him to address the weakness of the Japanese yen at a finance G-7 meeting. See also the December 14, 2006 letter from the chairman and ranking member of the Senate Banking Committee (Senators Dodd and Shelby) to Secretary Paulson pressing for Chinese currency reform and increased market access for American companies.

2. See also Hufbauer and Brunel (2007). For discussion of present trade politics, see Destler (2007). For earlier bills, see Hufbauer, Wong, and Sheth (2006).

reactive, rather than proactive, exhibiting the "fire alarm" rather than the "police patrol" pattern of oversight (McCubbins and Schwartz 1984, Epstein and O'Halloran 1995). They have sometimes, but not always, asked the right questions.

Congress has dropped the ball with respect to two substantive issues in particular. First, it has given far too little weight to the relative values of the key currencies (e.g., the dollar-euro rate during 1999–2000) and the value of the dollar on an effective basis. Second, its oversight of the emerging-market currencies, which are emphasized, has not given due consideration to *over*valuation as opposed to undervaluation. The Mexican peso and Asian financial crises demonstrated that overvalued currencies also pose important risks for the US economy.

Appendix 5A

Table 5A.1 Congressional hearings on exchange rate reports, 1988–2007

No.	Date	Title	Chamber and committee	Treasury witnesses	Outside witnesses	Members attending	Subjects of questions
1	May 5, 1989	First Annual Hearing on International Economic and Exchange Rate Policy	Senate Banking, 101st Congress, 1st Session	Nicholas F. Brady, secretary; David C. Mulford, under-secretary for international affairs	None	Riegle (D-MI), Sarbanes (D-MD), Dixon (D-IL), Kerry (D-MA), Garn (R-UT), Heinz (R-PA), Bond (R-MI), Roth (R-DE), and Pressler (R-SD)	▪ Jurisdiction (Super 301; GATT) ▪ Other than exchange rate manipulation ▪ Impact on agriculture ▪ Net foreign debt ▪ Antidumping actions ▪ Capital market liberalization (Japan)
2	May 12, 1989	Currency Manipulation	Senate Finance, Subcommittee on International Trade, 101st Congress, 1st Session	David C. Mulford, undersecretary	Allan I. Mendelowitz, GAO; John Williamson, IIE; and C. Fred Bergsten, IIE	Baucus (D-MT)	▪ Progress on negotiations with Korea and Taiwan ▪ Integrate trade with currency negotiations? ▪ Distinction between currency undervaluation and trade barriers
3	October 31, 1989	Treasury Department's Report on International Economic and Exchange Rate Policy	House Banking, Subcommittee on Development, Finance, Trade and Monetary Policy, 101st Congress, 1st Session	David C. Mulford, undersecretary	Manuel H. Johnson, Federal Reserve; Stephen Cooney, NAM; Robert Morris, USCIB; C. Randall Henning, IIE; Robert Solomon, Brookings; and John Williamson, IIE	Fauntroy (DC), LaFalce (D-NY), Leach (R-IA), McCandless (R-CA), Neal (D-MA), Saiki (R-HI), Ridge (R-PA), Kennedy II (D-MA), McMillen (D-MD), Hoagland (D-NE), Flake (R-AZ), and Pease (D-OH)	▪ Trade deficit, budget deficit ▪ Germany's trade surplus ▪ Strong dollar policy, yen-dollar, Deutsche mark-dollar ▪ Issue Treasury obligations in other currencies? ▪ Benefits of coordinated intervention ▪ "Manipulation" of the dollar ▪ Exchange Stabilization Fund (ESF) ▪ Treasury–Federal Reserve cooperation on intervention

(table continues next page)

Note: Hearings listed in this table are devoted in substantial measure to Treasury's exchange rate reports. Congressional committees also conducted a number of hearings that examined exchange rates and their impact on external balances and macroeconomic conditions but that did not specifically address Treasury's reports. The hearings listed here are thus a subset of a larger group that constitutes oversight of exchange rate policy broadly defined.

Table 5A.1 Congressional hearings on exchange rate reports, 1988–2007 (continued)

No.	Date	Title	Chamber and committee	Treasury witnesses	Outside witnesses	Members attending	Subjects of questions
4	November 16, 1989	Review of the Treasury's Second Annual Report on International Economic and Exchange Rate Policy	Senate Banking, Subcommittee on International Finance and Monetary Policy, 101st Congress, 1st Session	David C. Mulford, undersecretary	Manuel H. Johnson, vice chairman, Federal Reserve	Sarbanes (D-MD) and Heinz (R-PA)	• Negotiations with Korea • Tie manipulation to trade talks with Korea? • US, German, and Japanese interest rates • Domestic inflation and dollar policy • OECD versus G-7 and IMF as forums for policy coordination
5	April 19, 1990	Department of the Treasury's Report on International Economic and Exchange Rate Policy	Senate Banking, Subcommittee on International Finance and Monetary Policy, 101st Congress, 2nd Session	David C. Mulford, undersecretary	Horst Schulmann, IIF; and Edward L. Hudgins, Heritage Foundation	Sarbanes (D-MD), Heinz (R-PA), Dixon (D-IL), and Shelby (R-AL)	• Impact of German unification • Depreciation of yen • Japanese capital controls • Why China not cited in report • Effectiveness of G-7 meetings
6	May 9, 1990	Proposed US Participation in the European Bank for Reconstruction and Development (EBRD), and Update on Exchange Rate Report[a]	House Banking, Subcommittee on Development, Finance, Trade and Monetary Policy, 101st Congress, 2nd Session	David C. Mulford, undersecretary	None	Fauntroy (DC, chair)	• Trade deficit • Impact on jobs
7	August 14, 1990	Review of Treasury Department's Conduct of International Financial Policy	House Banking, Subcommittee on Development, Finance, Trade and Monetary Policy, 101st Congress, 2nd Session	David C. Mulford, undersecretary	Allan Mendelowitz, GAO; Alan Meltzer, Carnegie-Mellon University; Anna Schwartz, NBER; Martin Mayer; and Christopher Whalen, Whalen Co.	Gonzalez (D-TX)	• Subsidy to Mexico through Brady Plan (zero coupon bonds) • "Back-door schemes" through less developed countries' debt initiative and use of ESF • Amendment to ESF statute • Jurisdiction over management of foreign exchange reserves

No.	Date	Document	Committee/Session	Treasury witness	Outside witness	Senators	Topics
8	May 16, 1991	Treasury Department's Report on International Economic and Exchange Rate Policy	Senate Banking, Subcommittee on International Finance and Monetary Policy, 102nd Congress, 1st Session	David C. Mulford, undersecretary	C. Fred Bergsten, IIE	Sarbanes (D-MD), Riegle (D-MI), and Dixon (D-IL)	• Foreign versus domestic policy goals • China: manipulation versus most-favored nation (MFN) status • Strong dollar • G-7 interest rates (especially Japan compared with the United States) • Korea's and Taiwan's capital restrictions
9	November 12, 1991	Department of the Treasury's Report on International Economic and Exchange Rate Policy: 1991	Senate Banking, Subcommittee on International Finance and Monetary Policy, 102nd Congress, 1st Session	David C. Mulford, undersecretary	None	Sarbanes (D-MD)	• Korea, Taiwan, China • Manipulation definitional issues • Global economic growth • Trade deficit • Europe versus the United States on trade with China
10	May 12, 1992	Treasury Report on Exchange Rates and International Monetary Policy	Senate Banking, Subcommittee on International Finance and Monetary Policy, 102nd Congress, 2nd Session	David C. Mulford, undersecretary	None	Riegle (D-MI), Sarbanes (D-MD), Dixon (D-IL), Graham (D-FL), Sanford (D-NC), Wirth (D-CO), Mack (R-FL), Domenici (R-NM), and Kassebaum (R-KS)	• Korea, Taiwan, China • Trade surpluses and internal reforms • Brady debt reduction • Enterprise of the Americas Initiative • Russia Stabilization Fund and General Arrangements to Borrow
11	May 25, 1993	Treasury Department's Biannual Report on International Economic and Exchange Rate Policy	Senate Banking, Subcommittee on International Finance and Monetary Policy, 103rd Congress, 1st Session	Lawrence H. Summers, undersecretary	None	Riegle (D-MI), Mack (R-FL), and Sasser (D-TN)	• China: manipulation versus MFN • Russia: currency board? • China: Super 301 and/or Ex-Im Bank war chest? • Fair Trade in Financial Services Act (Japan) • Recession in Europe, Japan

(table continues next page)

Table 5A.1   Congressional hearings on exchange rate reports, 1988–2007 *(continued)*

No.	Date	Title	Chamber and committee	Treasury witnesses	Outside witnesses	Members attending	Subjects of questions
12	May 26, 1993	Small Business and the International Economy: Conditions for Operating at Home and Abroad	House Committee on Small Business, 103rd Congress, 1st Session	Lawrence H. Summers, undersecretary	None	LaFalce (D-NY), Meyers (R-KS), Ramstad (R-MN), Poshard (D-IL), Talent (R-MO), and Huffington (R-TX)	• Impact of exchange rate on small business exports • NAFTA • Export-led versus domestic demand-led growth in Japan • Japanese versus US current account • China: manipulation versus MFN
13	July 21, 1994	Treasury Department's Spring 1994 Report on International Economic and Exchange Rate Policy	Senate Banking, 103rd Congress, 2nd Session	Lawrence H. Summers, undersecretary	None	Riegle (D-MI), Sasser (D-TN), D'Amato (R-NY)[b], Bond (R-MI), Mack (R-FL), Domenici (R-NM), and Sarbanes (D-MD)	• China: manipulation versus MFN • US interest rates and capital account development • NAFTA • Decline of yen
14	May 1, 2002	US Department of the Treasury's Report to Congress on International Economic and Exchange Rate Policy	Senate Banking, 107th Congress, 2nd Session	Paul H. O'Neill, secretary	Richard L. Trumka, AFL-CIO; Jerry J. Jasinowski, NAM; Bob Stallman, AFBF; C. Fred Bergsten, IIE; Ernest H. Preeg, Manufacturers Alliance; and Steve H. Hanke, Johns Hopkins University	Sarbanes (D-MD), Bunning (R-KY), Johnson (D-SD), Miller (D-GA), Corzine (D-NJ), Akaka (D-HI), Gramm (R-TX), and Ensign (R-NV)	• Jobs • Foreign holdings of Treasury securities • Importance of the concept of the current account balance • Manipulation definitional issues • Dubai communiqué: need a new Plaza agreement? • Domestic saving rate and capital account

	Date	Title	Committee	Treasury witness	Other witnesses	Issues raised
15	October 1, 2003	China's Exchange Rate Regime and Its Effects on the US Economy	House Financial Services Committee, International Subcommittee, 108th Congress, 1st Session	John B. Taylor, undersecretary for international affairs	Rep. Mark Green (R-WS); Rep. Phil English (R-PA); Grant D. Aldonas, undersecretary, Department of Commerce; Franklin J. Vargo, NAM; and Morris Goldstein, IIE	• Jobs, interest rates, consumer prices • Foreign holdings of Treasury securities • HR 3058 (China Act): tariffs equal to the margin of manipulation • Renminbi value and US exports • Timetable for floating • China's capital flows
16	October 30–31, 2003	US-China Economic Relations and China's Role in the Global Economy (Panels 1 and 2)	House Ways and Means Committee, 108th Congress, 1st Session	John B. Taylor, undersecretary	Gregory N. Mankiw, CEA; Josette S. Shiner, Office of USTR; Douglas Holtz-Eakin, CBO; Loren Yager, GAO; and Robert A. Rogowski, US International Trade Commission	• Why no reference to Japan in report? • Trade deficit • Timetable for floating • Foreign holdings of Treasury securities • Efficacy of tariff legislation • Impact of manipulation on manufacturing jobs • Relationship between nominal and real rates
17	October 30, 2003	Treasury Department's Report to Congress on International Economic and Exchange Rate Policies	Senate Banking, 108th Congress, 1st Session	John W. Snow, secretary	None	• China: interim one-off revaluation versus flexibility? • Schumer-Graham proposed 27.5 percent tariff on China imports • China: internal reforms • Reports more prescriptive? • Super 301, multilateral response (IMF, WTO)?

(table continues next page)

Table 5A.1 Congressional hearings on exchange rate reports, 1988–2007 *(continued)*

No.	Date	Title	Chamber and committee	Treasury witnesses	Outside witnesses	Members attending	Subjects of questions
18	May 26, 2005	Report to the Congress on International Economic and Exchange Rate Policies	Senate Banking, 109th Congress, 1st Session	John W. Snow, secretary	None	Shelby (R-AL), Bennett (R-UT), Allard (R-CO), Bunning (R-KY), Crapo (R-ID), Dole (R-NC), Hagel (R-NE), Sarbanes (D-MD), Schumer (D-NY), Bayh (D-IN), Carper (D-DE), and Stabenow (D-MI)	• Trade deficit and jobs • State Department authorization bill amendments (China) • Renminbi linchpin for the region? • HR 782 and S 796 (to amend Tariff Act of 1930 and clarify currency manipulation in Omnibus Act of 1988)
19	May 18, 2006	International Economic and Exchange Rate Policies	Senate Banking, 109th Congress, 2nd Session	John W. Snow, secretary	None	Shelby (R-AL), Bennett (R-UT), Allard (R-CO), Bunning (R-KY), Crapo (R-ID), Dole (R-NC), Schumer (D-NY), Bayh (D-IN), Carper (D-DE), and Johnson (D-SD)	• Trade deficit and jobs • Manipulation definitional issues • Fuel exporters and current account deficit • Budget deficit • China's internal reforms to boost domestic demand?
20	January 31, 2007	Department of Treasury Report on the International Economic and Exchange Rate Policy and US-China Strategic Economic Dialogue	Senate Banking, 110th Congress, 1st Session	Henry M. Paulson, secretary	Richard Trumka, AFL-CIO; Michael Campbell, NAM; Albert Keidel, Carnegie Endowment for International Peace; and C. Fred Bergsten, PIIE	Dodd (D-CT), Shelby (R-AL), Carper (D-DE), Sununu (R-NH), Bayh (D-IN), Bunning (R-KY), Brown (D-OH), Bennett (R-UT), Reed (D-RI), and Allard (R-CO)	• Trade deficit and jobs • How to measure progress on currency issue; specific steps • Chinese holding of US debt • Is manipulation a subsidy? • Dispute resolution at WTO • Long-term structural problems in China • Impact on agriculture and high-tech sectors

#	Date	Title	Committee/Session	Administration witnesses	Other witnesses	Members	Issues
21	March 28, 2007	US-China Economic Relations	Senate Finance, 110th Congress, 1st Session	None	Charles Schumer (D-NY); Lindsey Graham (R-SC); Stephen Roach, Morgan Stanley; Eswar Prasad, Cornell University; Morris Goldstein, PIIE; and John Makin, PAEI	Baucus (D-MT), Bunning (R-KY), Stabenow (D-MI), Smith (R-OR), and Grassley (R-IA)	• Manipulation definitional issues • Liberalization of capital flows and financial-sector reforms • Real effective undervaluation of renminbi • IMF inaction over currencies • Design of international code of conduct on exchange rate policy • Lack of focus on Japan
22	May 9, 2007	Currency Manipulation and Its Effects on US Business and Workers	House Ways and Means Committee, Trade Subcommittee; House Energy and Commerce Committee, Trade Subcommittee; House Financial Services Committee, Technology Subcommittee, 110th Congress, 1st Session	Mark Sobel, deputy assistant secretary, international monetary and financial policy	Stephen Claeys, Department of Commerce; Daniel Brinza, assistant USTR; and Donald L. Evans, former secretary, Department of Commerce	Levin (D-MI), Rush (D-IL), Gutierrez (D-IL), Ryan (R-OH), Herger (R-CA), Stearns (R-FL), Sherman (D-CA), and Brady (R-TX)	• IMF to improve exchange rate surveillance • Use annual review process in the WTO to address manipulation • Is manipulation a subsidy? • China's domestic effects from undervalued renminbi • Manipulation definitional issues • China's broader financial reforms • Jurisdiction within administration
23	May 23, 2007	US Economic Relations with China	Senate Banking, Subcommittee on Security and International Trade and Finances, 110th Congress, 1st Session	None	Morris Goldstein, PIIE; Robert S. Nichols, Financial Services Forum; David Hartquist, China Currency Coalition; Patrick A. Mulloy; George Mason University; and John W. Nolan, Steel Dynamics, Inc.	Bayh (D-IN), Bunning (R-KY), and Casey (D-PA)	• Impact on manufacturing sector • Impact of Chinese practices on other East Asian countries • Is manipulation a subsidy? • WTO, IMF, or unilateral approach to manipulation? • Manipulation versus misalignment • Chinese foreign direct investment and portfolio investment in the United States • Domestic demand in China

(table continues next page)

Table 5A.1 Congressional hearings on exchange rate reports, 1988–2007 *(continued)*

No.	Date	Title	Chamber and committee	Treasury witnesses	Outside witnesses	Members attending	Subjects of questions
24	June 20, 2007	The State of the International Financial Services System	House Financial Services Committee, 110th Congress, 1st Session	Henry M. Paulson, secretary	None	Frank (D-MA), Bachus (R-AL), Gutierrez (D-IL), Paul (R-TX), Maloney (D-NY), Waters (D-CA), Royce (R-CA), Shays (R-CA), Ackerman (D-NY), Campbell (R-CA), D. Moore (D-KS), Garrett (R-NJ), Watt (D-NC), Bachman (R-MN), Green (D-TX), G. Moore (D-WI), and Davis (D-TN)	• China's capital controls and financial sector liberalization • Manipulation of renminbi and definitional issues • Costs versus benefits of trade remedies against manipulation • Decline of the dollar • US versus foreign saving rates • Foreign national and China's holdings of US debt

a. Devoted mostly to discussion of the EBRD.
b. Senator D'Amato did not appear but submitted a prepared statement.

Table 5A.2 Exchange rate bills submitted to the 110th Congress, 1st Session, January–December 2007

No.	Sponsors	Bill no.	Date introduced	Committee of jurisdiction	Substantive measures
1	Dodd (D-CT), Shelby (R-AL), Bayh (D-IN), Bunning (R-KY), Carper (D-DE), Brown (D-OH), Casey (D-PA), and Stabenow (D-MI)	S 1677	June 12, 2007	Senate Banking	**Title:** Currency Reform and Financial Markets Access Act of 2007 **Synopsis:** To recognize and remedy currency manipulation by China and other countries, promotes Treasury's role in enhancing the competitiveness of US financial services firms. **Reporting requirements:** Requires the Treasury to submit a detailed plan of action to the Congress within 30 days of a finding of manipulation; requires the Treasury to annually monitor and report to the Senate Banking and the House Financial Services Committees on market access barriers for US financial services firms, to identify challenges, and to develop plans to address those barriers; requires the Treasury's initial report to include the status of the US-China Strategic Economic Dialogue (SED) as it relates to financial services firms. This would become the only congressionally required report on the progress of the SED. **Manipulation:** Clarifies the definition to identify countries that have both a material global current account surplus and a significant bilateral trade surplus with the United States and that have engaged in prolonged, one-way intervention as currency manipulators. Abandons intent as material to the finding of manipulation. **Sanctions:** Requires Treasury to file a World Trade Organization (WTO) Article XV case if manipulation is not remedied within 300 days; the Treasury must immediately seek International Monetary Fund (IMF) consultations when manipulation is found; and requires Treasury to use its voice and vote at the IMF accordingly. President can waive requirement to pursue WTO case if vital economic and security interests are threatened. **Comment:** (1) Provides for an expedited joint resolution of disapproval by Congress, led by either the Senate Banking or House Financial Services Committee, when Treasury declines to cite manipulation; (2) Alternates the secretary's testimony on reports between the House Financial Services and Senate Banking Committees.

(table continues next page)

Table 5A.2 Exchange rate bills submitted to the 110th Congress, 1st Session, January–December 2007 *(continued)*

No.	Sponsors	Bill no.	Date introduced	Committee of jurisdiction	Substantive measures
2	Baucus (D-MT), Grassley (R-IA), Schumer (D-NY), Graham (R-SC), and others	S 1607	June 13, 2007	Senate Finance	**Title:** Currency Exchange Rate Oversight Reform Act of 2007 **Synopsis:** To provide for identification of misaligned currency, require action to correct the misalignment, and for other purposes. **Reporting requirements:** Creates a new body, an Advisory Committee on International Exchange Rate Policy, with which Treasury must consult during the development of its report. **Manipulation:** Two categories of currencies: (1) a general category of "fundamentally misaligned currencies," and (2) a select category of currencies for "priority action" whose misalignments are caused by policy actions of the issuing government. **Sanctions:** (1) Immediately upon designating a currency as fundamentally misaligned, the Treasury shall initiate bilateral consultations to redress. For currencies designated for priority action, Treasury shall also seek the advice of the IMF and the support of third governments and shall oppose changes in IMF governance that benefit the designated country. (2) If the government issuing a currency for priority action has not adopted remedial measures within 90 days, the following measures shall be taken: (a) reflect currency undervaluation in dumping calculations for products of the designated country, (b) forbid federal procurement of its goods and services (unless the country concerned is a member of the WTO Agreement on Government Procurement), (c) request the IMF to engage the country in special consultations, (d) forbid Overseas Private Investment Corporation financing or insurance projects for the country, and (e) oppose new multilateral bank financing for projects. (3) After 360 days: (a) US Trade Representative (USTR) shall request consultations with the issuing government in the WTO and (b) the Treasury shall consult with the Federal Reserve, other monetary authorities, and the IMF on remedial intervention. **Comment:** (1) The president could waive countermeasures for inaction, with justification, if they would harm US national security or the vital economic interest; however, Congress can disapprove the waiver; (2) The banking and finance committees of both houses could hold hearings on the exchange rate reports with the secretary; (3) Would repeal the exchange rate provisions of the 1988 Act, replace them, and eliminate the word "manipulation."

3	Bunning (R-KY), Bayh (D-IN), Casey (D-PA), Levin (D-MI), Snowe (R-ME), and Stabenow (D-MI)	S 796	March 7, 2007	Senate Finance	**Comment:** The same as HR 782.
4	Dorgan (D-ND), Brown (D-OH), and Graham (R-SC)	S 571	February 13, 2007	Senate Finance	**Title:** None provided **Synopsis:** To withdraw normal trade relations treatment from, and apply certain provisions of title IV of the Trade Act of 1974 to, the products of China. **Reporting requirements:** No change. **Manipulation:** No change. **Sanctions:** Proposes a withdrawal of normal trade relations treatment from China. **Comment:** Normal trade relations treatment may be extended to products of China only in accordance with the provisions of sections 401 to 409 of the Trade Act of 1974.
5	Rockefeller (D-WV)	S 364	January 23, 2007	Senate Finance	**Title:** Strengthening America's Trade Laws Act **Synopsis:** A bill to strengthen United States trade laws and for other purposes. **Reporting requirements:** No change. **Manipulation:** Title III, section 302: treatment of exchange rate manipulation as countervailable subsidy under title VII of the Tariff Act of 1930; section 771 of the Tariff Act of 1930 is amended to include the definition of exchange rate manipulation. **Sanctions:** Exchange rate manipulation therefore pursuant to dispute settlement in WTO, amendments to which are proposed in title I of the law, inter alia containing establishment of a congressional advisory commission on WTO dispute settlement. **Comment:** Title II modifies criteria for designating and revoking the nonmarket economy country status. A country found to be engaged in exchange rate manipulation may have status of a market economy, a nonmarket economy, or a combination thereof.
6	Stabenow (D-MI)	S 1021	March 28, 2007	Senate Finance	**Title:** Japan Currency Manipulation Act **Synopsis:** To address the exchange rate misalignment of the Japanese yen with respect to the US dollar, and for other purposes. **Reporting requirements:** Every 180 days, the Secretary of the Treasury shall submit a report on currency intervention by the government of Japan

(table continues next page)

Table 5A.2 Exchange rate bills submitted to the 110th Congress, 1st Session, January–December 2007 (continued)

No.	Sponsors	Bill no.	Date introduced	Committee of jurisdiction	Substantive measures
6 (cont'd)					with respect to the dollar and other currencies since 2000, and on any efforts to create exchange rate misalignment since March 2004; for each incident described in the report, a justification should be provided for lack of activity mandated under (1) Exchange Rates and International Economic Policy Act of 1988, (2) title III of the Trade Act of 1974, and (3) section 2102(c) of the Bipartisan Trade Promotion Authority Act of 2002; every 180 days, the secretary shall report to the Senate Finance Committee and House Ways and Means Committee on progress toward decreasing and eliminating the misalignment of the yen with respect to the dollar. **Manipulation:** "Exchange rate misalignment" means the undervaluation of the yen as a result of the protracted large-scale currency intervention by or at the direction of the government of Japan. **Sanctions:** Secretary, in consultation with the Council of Economic Advisors, shall initiate consultation with the government of Japan; call for the special meeting at the IMF; in case of intervention, the Secretary shall take immediate action unilaterally, bilaterally, or multilaterally. **Comment:** Proposal for a joint United States–European Union plan to address the misalignment of the yen, by raising the issue at each meeting of G-7 finance ministers and G-7 leaders until the misalignment is removed.
7	Stabenow (D-MI), Graham (R-SC), and Levin (D-MI)	S 445	January 31, 2007	Senate Finance	**Title:** Trade Prosecutor Act **Synopsis:** To establish the position of trade enforcement officer (TEO) and a Trade Enforcement Division in the Office of the USTR, to require identification of trade enforcement priorities, and for other purposes. **Reporting requirements:** No change. **Manipulation:** Citing the country as a manipulator under section 3005 of the Omnibus Trade and Competitiveness Act of 1988 qualifies as a priority foreign country trade practice to be addressed by the TEO. **Sanctions:** TEO to seek satisfactory resolution with the country or countries engaging in manipulation under the auspices of the WTO, pursuant to a bilateral or regional trade agreement to which the United States is a party or by any other means. A satisfactory resolution may include elimination of manipulation or providing for compensatory benefits.
8	Camp (R-MI) and Jones (D-OH)	HR 1278	January 3, 2007	House Ways and Means	**Comment:** The same as S 445.

	Sponsor	Bill	Date	Committee	Description
9	Davis (D-AL) and English (R-PA)	HR 1229	February 27, 2007	House Ways and Means	**Title:** Nonmarket Economy Trade Remedy Act of 2007 **Synopsis:** To amend title VII of the Tariff Act of 1930 so that the provisions relating to countervailing duties apply to nonmarket-economy countries, and for other purposes. **Reporting requirements:** No change. **Manipulation:** No change. **Sanctions:** Section 701 of the Tariff Act of 1930 is amended to make nonmarket economies acceptable for countervailing duty cases; section 771 is amended to allow the use of alternative methodologies for administrative authority to calculate the benefits conferred with respect to countervailable subsidies in China; if conditions prevailing in China are not available as appropriate benchmarks, conditions and terms outside China (those of the WTO) are to be used. **Comment:** Provides that a determination by the administration to revoke a country's nonmarket economy status must be approved by Congress in the form of a joint resolution, to be considered under expedited procedure and without opportunity for amendment; requires the US International Trade Commission to conduct a study of Chinese government intervention practices and to update the report annually until 2017.
10	English (R-PA), Hayes (R-NC), and Reynolds (R-NY)	HR 321	January 9, 2007	House Ways and Means	**Title:** Currency Harmonization Initiative Through Neutralizing Action Act of 2005 **Synopsis:** To require the secretary of the Treasury to analyze and report on the exchange rate policies of China and to require that additional tariffs be imposed on China's products on the basis of the rate of manipulation of the rate of exchange between the renminbi and the US dollar. **Reporting requirements:** Annual report by the Treasury to House Ways and Means and Senate Finance Committees about the exchange rate policies of China. **Manipulation:** No change. **Sanctions:** Manipulation-neutralizing tariffs (above).
11	Kaptur (D-OH)	HR 1958	April 19, 2007	House Ways and Means	**Comment:** The same as S 571.
12	Ryan (D-OH), Hunter (R-CA), and 31 other cosponsors	HR 782	January 31, 2007	House Ways and Means	**Title:** Fair Currency Act of 2007 **Synopsis:** To amend title VII of the Tariff Act of 1930 to make exchange rate misalignment by any foreign nation a countervailable export subsidy, to apply countervailing duties to nonmarket economies, to amend the Exchange Rates and International Economic Policy Coordination Act of 1988 to clarify the definition of manipulation, and for other purposes.

(table continues next page)

Table 5A.2 Exchange rate bills submitted to the 110th Congress, 1st Session, January–December 2007 *(continued)*

No.	Sponsors	Bill no.	Date introduced	Committee of jurisdiction	Substantive measures
12 *(cont'd)*					**Reporting requirements:** Modest change, inclusion of "fundamental misalignment" definition. **Manipulation:** Adds the concept of "fundamental misalignment," defining it as a "material sustained disparity between the observed levels of an effective exchange rate for a currency and the corresponding levels of an effective exchange rate for that currency that would be consistent with fundamental macroeconomic conditions based on a generally accepted economic rationale." Treasury would negotiate with countries that manipulate or have fundamentally misaligned currencies. **Sanctions:** Fundamental misalignment would become countervailable under Title VII of the Tariff Act of 1930; misalignment is to be considered with respect to market disruption under chapter 2 of title IV of the Trade Act of 1974; officials must oppose changes to the governance of international financial institutions that benefit a country whose currency is designated as manipulated.
13	Ryan (D-OH), Hunter (R-CA), and 64 other cosponsors	HR 2942	June 28, 2007	House Ways and Means	**Title:** Currency Reform for Fair Trade Act of 2007 **Synopsis:** A bill to provide for identification of misaligned currency, require action to correct misalignment, and for other purposes. **Reporting requirements:** Modest change, inclusion of "fundamental misalignment" definition **Manipulation:** Substitutes the concept of "fundamental misalignment," defining it as a "situation in which a country's prevailing real effective exchange rate is undervalued relative to the country's equilibrium real effective exchange rate, and the Secretary determines that the amount of the undervaluation exceeds 5 percent and has consistently exceeded 5 percent in the 18-month period preceding the date of the calculation of the amount of the undervaluation." Treasury would designate misaligned currencies for priority action if they satisfy certain criteria, including intervention. **Sanctions:** Fundamental misalignment under this definition becomes countervailable under title VII of the Tariff Act of 1930; the margin of undervaluation could be included in the calculation of antidumping duties; would provide for countervailing duties against nonmarket economies; USTR to request consultations in the WTO; opposes any international financial institution governance changes that benefit a designated country, among other countermeasures. **Comment:** Establishes an Advisory Committee on International Exchange Rate Policy.

#	Sponsor	Bill	Date	Committee	Details
14	Spratt (D-SC) and Myrick (R-NC)	HR 1002	February 12, 2007	House Ways and Means	**Title:** None provided **Synopsis:** To authorize appropriate action if the negotiations with China regarding its undervalued currency and currency manipulation are not successful. **Reporting requirements:** No change. **Manipulation:** No change. **Sanctions:** Imposes an additional duty rate of 27.5 percent ad valorem on any article imported into the United States that is the growth, product, or manufacture of China unless the president certifies to Congress that (1) China is no longer manipulating the exchange rate between its currency and the US dollar in order to prevent an effective balance of payments and gain an unfair international trade advantage; and (2) China's currency is valued in accordance with accepted market-based trading policies. **Comment:** Directs the secretary of the Treasury to begin negotiations with China for adoption of a market-based currency valuation system.
15	Tancredo (R-CO)	HR 571	January 18, 2007	House Ways and Means	**Title:** None provided **Synopsis:** To require additional tariffs be imposed on products of any nonmarket economy country until the president certifies to Congress that the country is a market economy, and to direct the secretary of the Treasury to deposit the amounts generated from those tariffs into the Social Security trust funds. **Reporting requirements:** No change. **Manipulation:** No change. **Sanctions:** Imposes additional tariffs on any article that is the growth, product, or manufacture of a nonmarket economy country and is imported directly or indirectly into the United States: (1) a rate of duty of 5 percent ad valorem during the first year, and (2) additional duty of 1 percent ad valorem in each succeeding year. **Comment:** "Nonmarket country" applies to Albania, Armenia, Azerbaijan, Belarus, Cambodia, China, Georgia, Kyrgyzstan, Laos, Moldova, Tajikistan, Turkmenistan, Ukraine, Uzbekistan, Vietnam, Cuba, and North Korea; and any other country the president determines is a nonmarket country as defined in section 771 of the Tariff Act of 1930; China shall not be construed to include Taiwan.
16	Knollenberg (R-MI)	HR 2886	June 27, 2007	House Ways and Means, House Financial Services	**Comment:** The same as S 1021.

6

Recommendations

With most current legislative proposals motivated by congressional discontent with Chinese exchange rate policy, there is a danger that Congress will lose sight of the broader purposes of the Exchange Rates and International Economic Policy Coordination Act of 1988. As legislation makes its way through Congress and toward the president's desk, legislators should keep the broader aspects of US external monetary policy on the agenda: the overall value of the dollar, especially against other key currencies, the risks of external deficits, prudential limits to external debt, the dollar's role in the international monetary system, and the mandate to cooperate with international partners.

With respect to these matters, as well as currency manipulation, the mechanism by which policymakers are held to account should be improved in several respects. The present mandate with respect to exchange rate policy is partial and should be made more complete, and the standards for assessing whether Treasury has satisfied it should be clarified. Treasury should be more timely, complete, and forthcoming in the reporting process. And Congress should be more systematic and diligent in its review of Treasury's performance relative to its mandate. These goals should be advanced through several specific measures.

Preparation of the Reports

Treasury should change its general approach to the reports even if there is no change in the law. Too often in the past, Treasury's approach could best be described as "legalistic minimalism." The approach has become substantially more forthcoming since 2005. But Treasury can further embrace the reporting process, using it to explain, defend, and advance its policy more fully, mold the terms of public and academic discourse, and signal its position to foreign governments and international organizations such as the International Monetary Fund (IMF).

Specifically, first of all, Treasury can provide more (but not necessarily complete) information on past events, negotiations, and interlocutors. It can provide more details on negotiations in the G-7 and other financial forums, as well as the bilateral surveillance consultations with the IMF. It can be more candid about the positions of other players on policy questions of interest to the United States, such as the reluctance of the Europeans to press China more strongly for revaluation prior to 2007 (Taylor 2007, Henning 2007a). The department must safeguard the confidence of its foreign counterparts, but this condition nonetheless leaves room for more transparency.

Second, the reports would benefit from more analysis about the relationships between the exchange rate and macroeconomic policies, the endogeneity of the exchange rate, and the instances when the exchange rate becomes disconnected from the economic fundamentals (as had the dollar/euro rate in the second half of 2000). Given the importance of the US federal budget deficit for the current account balance, although the relationship is not one-for-one, it is especially important that Treasury present deeper analysis of this connection. In this regard, Treasury could provide more analysis of the economic tradeoffs involved in policy decisions. A clear statement about tradeoffs would be a contribution to the policy debate, even if the report were agnostic on how the tradeoff should be decided.

Third, Treasury must revise the criteria by which it determines manipulation, regardless of whether it is required to do so by changes in the law, and should do so along the lines suggested below.

Fourth, because sustained overvaluation can pose risks for the US economy that are also substantial, as the Mexican peso and Asian financial crises showed, Treasury should treat such cases even though the 1988 Act might not explicitly require it to do so. The focus on undervaluation in the Act is more relevant at present, given the persistent US current account deficit and the substantial buildup of external debt. But the external position will evolve, and examining cases of overvaluation as well as undervaluation would give greater balance to the reports. Owing to the risk of sparking a crisis, Treasury must admittedly be more careful and nuanced in public statements about cases of overvaluation. But judicious treatment could nonetheless steer a middle course between silence and provoking a crisis (Goldstein 1997).

Finally, Treasury should be more punctual in the submission of its reports to Congress. Of the 39 reports required by the Act since October 1988, four were missed completely and folded into subsequent reports.

None of the 35 reports that were submitted were received before the technical deadlines of October 15 and April 15, and only 13 of those reports were received less than a month late (table 4A.1). The overshooting of the deadline is all the more significant when the report is lagged.

General Objectives

Although Congress has delegated exchange rate policy to the Treasury and Federal Reserve, as discussed at the outset, it has not specified a comprehensive mandate for these agencies in US law. The authors of the 1988 Act intended to make the objective of a "more appropriate and sustainable balance in the current account" the fulcrum against which to increase the accountability of the Treasury (US Congress, 1988, 840; US House of Representatives 1987). In the event, however, the statement of policy in the Act proved to be insufficient as a guide for evaluating whether the department lived up to the mandate. This and other legislated objectives amount to a patchwork of partial mandates that, taken as a whole, is incomplete. The accountability process would benefit from clarifying the general objectives of US policy in this area and the standards by which Treasury's execution of policy could be assessed.

This new, broad mandate would place the exchange rate in a general equilibrium framework in which its essential purpose would be conceived as bringing equilibrium to the domestic and global markets in goods, services, and capital, or, more precisely, to the sum of these markets as they operate through the balance of payments. The exchange rate and its movements, in this conventional conceptualization, would reconcile ex ante incompatibilities between the domestic economy and the world economy. In the first instance, policy would allow the exchange rate to operate smoothly in this role. This objective will sometimes imply that the United States can make fiscal and monetary policy choices primarily on domestic macroeconomic considerations and treat the exchange rate as the residual. At other times, however, US officials cannot uncritically accept whatever exchange rates the markets might yield. US policymakers should not simply treat the exchange rate as a residual at present and, assuming the US economy continues to be progressively internationalized, they will be able to do so less often in the future than they have done in the past.

Policymakers, in particular, must become proactive with respect to the exchange rate in at least three circumstances.[1] First, even when capital markets might be willing to finance large current account deficits in

---

1. The literature on this subject is broad. See Williamson (2000, 2007), among other useful works.

the short term, such deficits might not be sustainable in the long term, and the buildup of external debt could be risky or inappropriate. Prudential limits on these external variables, with the exchange rate serving as the intermediate variable, should guide domestic choices on fiscal and monetary policies (and the macroeconomic policy choices of partners). Second, foreign exchange markets sometimes become unhinged from the economic fundamentals at home and abroad. When exchange rates become "exogenously determined," in the jargon of some economists, there may be a case for government action in the markets, directly through declarations or intervention, or indirectly via changes in macroeconomic policy. Third, when foreign governments intervene directly or indirectly, the exchange rate is, by definition, not fully market-determined. In such cases, US policymakers must consider whether foreign intervention is consistent with the interests of the US and world economies and, if they find that it is not, they should consider countervailing action (discussed below).

In its general mandate, Congress should make clear that it expects the executive to (1) assess whether these circumstances apply and, when it finds that they do, (2) recommend or take appropriate action. This would clarify the standards by which Treasury's broad mandate would be assessed and serve as a context for the specific mandate to target manipulation.

Current Account Balances and Real Effective Exchange Rates

The 1988 Act gave too much emphasis to bilateral trade imbalances between the United States and countries whose governments manipulate their currencies. International fragmentation of the production process and multilateralization of trade make bilateral imbalances nearly meaningless. Any basic university course in international economics will teach that a country's overall current account balance should be the focus of policy analysis. China is a case in point: a more substantial appreciation of the renminbi is desirable, from the standpoint of both China and the United States, because it would reduce China's large and growing global current account surplus and reduce the US current account deficit, not because of its impact on the bilateral imbalance with the United States. The reduction in the current account imbalance, not the bilateral imbalance, could raise American growth and employment and reduce Chinese overheating and inflation. Revision of the Act should shift the emphasis toward the overall current account balance when assessing manipulation and initiating subsequent negotiations.

As a consequence of placing the primary focus on the overall current account balance, findings of manipulation should focus on the real effective exchange rate rather than bilateral exchange rates. The real effective rate determines that balance more than any bilateral rate and captures competitiveness vis-à-vis third countries. If a currency that is found to be manipulated subsequently appreciates against the dollar but depreciates against the euro similarly, to choose a real-world example, global adjustment will not be served.

Emphasizing the current account balance could conceivably place the United States in the position of finding manipulation on the part of a country with whom the United States is not running a bilateral trade deficit, although such cases are not likely to be common. The United States would not, however, be advancing the interests of other countries at its own expense by initiating negotiations with such a country. Multilateral trade and capital flows bind the US external balance to that of manipulators and third countries inextricably. Because combating manipulation would facilitate global adjustment, including of the US current account, the United States would in fact be advancing its interests even in this case. That the United States would also be acting in the general global interest is a compelling reason to continue to vest the quest against manipulation primarily with the IMF. But that does not mean that the United States should not act when the IMF is not able to act or is unwilling to do so.

Manipulation

Some of the pieces of legislation currently under consideration by Congress introduce the concept of "misalignment" as well as "manipulation." It would not be desirable to completely replace the latter with the former, for two reasons. First, the criteria for defining manipulation are generally more concrete than those for misalignment. While some instances of misalignment can be clearly identified, others do not command scientific consensus. Second, a country can experience a misalignment without being responsible for it. In many cases the exchange rate has simply lost its moorings, becoming unhinged from the economic fundamentals. While it might be desirable for governments to act to bring the rate into alignment in such cases, requiring governments to do so would be tantamount to introducing a new exchange rate regime and is well beyond the intent of Congress at the moment. A country should have to be shown to (1) manipulate the exchange rate and (2) maintain a misalignment to become the target of US authorities for negotiations and possible countermeasures.

"Manipulation" should also be defined more clearly. The new language should be broadly consistent with the spirit of the IMF language without becoming immobilizing through obscure and unnecessary requirements about intent. Although it must give members "the benefit of any reasonable doubt," the IMF cannot simply take a government's statement of intent at face value. Ultimately, as the IMF general counsel has recently reiterated and the new guidelines confirm, the Fund itself must reach its own "objective" conclusion on the matter (IMF 2006, 2007). The US government must do the same. The new US legislation can reinforce the IMF, contribute to the smooth operation of the international monetary system, and enhance Treasury accountability to Congress by closing the loophole for exchange rate manipulation created by emphasizing intent. US legislation should target countries that manipulate simply "with the effect of preventing balance of payments adjustment."

US legislation should follow the IMF Guidelines for Exchange Rate Policy, which were revised in June 2007 (see appendix C; for the full document, see IMF 2007). Intended to operationalize the Article IV obligations, those guidelines specify four principles and seven policy actions that guide members with respect to intervention, manipulation, and exchange rate policy generally and could indicate a need for special consultations between a member and the Fund. One of the indicators, foreign exchange intervention, deserves special emphasis, while the remaining indicators should stay as part of a separate basket. Thus, new legislation should provide for the finding of manipulation in one of two ways.

First, foreign exchange intervention that (1) is large in scale, (2) is protracted over two or three years, (3) is consistently in one direction, and (4) perpetuates or accentuates a significant current account imbalance should alone qualify as manipulation. Such intervention would clearly indicate that the relevant monetary authority was preventing the currency from moving toward a rate that would contribute to current account adjustment.[2] This criterion has the benefit of concreteness, avoids debates about intent, and focuses on a dominant instrument by which some monetary authorities have blocked adjustment in practice. But this criterion has the disadvantage of being relatively narrow; once it were adopted, some governments might be tempted to evade a manipulation designation by relying more heavily on other means of managing the exchange rate. So legislation should provide for manipulation to be found through a second route as well.

The second route would be a basket of the remaining indicators in the IMF guidelines, which would apply when a fundamental exchange rate misalignment is found. The presence of one or more of the following could create a presumption that manipulation had taken place:

- an unsustainable level of official or quasi-official borrowing (by a deficit country) or lending (by a surplus country),

- restrictions or incentives on current transactions or capital inflows or outflows,

---

2. Relatedly, see John Williamson's reference rate proposal (2007).

- monetary or financial policies that provide abnormal encouragement or discouragement to capital flows,

- large and prolonged current account imbalances, and

- large external vulnerabilities arising from private capital flows.

Legislation should mandate that Treasury assess the key potential offenders along these presumptive indicators within a comprehensive analysis of the country's macroeconomic situation. Although Treasury should not be directed to apply the indicators mechanistically, placing them within the law would (1) foster convergence with IMF guidelines, (2) create more consistency on the criteria used in the exchange rate reports, and (3) make it more difficult for the report to avoid a manipulation finding in blatant cases. Finally, if Congress continues to be dissatisfied with the application of manipulation criteria, it is perfectly within its constitutional powers to consider delegating the job to another agency.

Countermeasures

How the United States should respond to a government that is found to manipulate its currency but persists is perhaps the most contentious aspect of the current batch of legislative proposals. Simply having the Treasury plead for appreciation in negotiations is too weak. But the original Schumer-Graham 27.5 percent across-the-board tariff was too blunt and was inconsistent with US obligations in the World Trade Organization (WTO). Several bills proposed during 2005–07 would provide for intermediate sanctions, including antidumping and countervailing duties, WTO cases, and the blocking of governance reforms in the IMF that could benefit manipulators (table 5A.2).

Currency undervaluation has effects on trade and current account balances that are similar to a tax on imports and a subsidy to exports of like amount.[3] A 20 percent real effective undervaluation of a currency, for example, essentially subsidizes the issuing country's exports by 20 percent and taxes its imports similarly. In principle, the United States could redress part of the competitiveness consequences of such an undervaluation by levying a tariff of the same size on its imports from the country in

---

3. For a discussion of Chinese currency undervaluation as an effective subsidy, see Ben S. Bernanke, speech entitled "The Chinese Economy: Progress and Challenges" at the Chinese Academy of Social Sciences, Beijing, December 15, 2006. See also C. Fred Bergsten, statement before the Hearing on US Economic Relations with China: Strategies and Options on Exchange Rates and Market Access, Subcommittee on Security and International Trade and Finance, Committee on Banking, Housing and Urban Affairs, United States Senate, Washington, May 23, 2007.

question. Several proposed bills aim to do this by adding the margin of undervaluation to antidumping and countervailing duties.

However, there are several caveats. First, such measures would do little to redress the competitiveness disadvantage faced by US exporters. Second, antidumping and countervailing duties are subject to multilateral discipline, and WTO rules govern them differently. Some analysts thus prefer challenging China's currency practices in the WTO on the basis of Article XV, section 4, which states that members "shall not, by exchange action, frustrate the intent of the provisions" of the General Agreement on Tariffs and Trade (GATT). Gary Hufbauer and Claire Brunel (2008) find that incorporating the margin of undervaluation into antidumping penalties would be less vulnerable to objections by China in the WTO than doing so for countervailing duties. But they conclude that such measures, or bringing an Article XV section 4 case against China in the WTO, would be best justified as a lever to prompt more forceful action by the IMF.

The merits of proposed countermeasures should be assessed in a broad, multilateral context. Foreign exchange intervention on the scale in which Chinese authorities have engaged creates large distortions in the international monetary and trade system. Their intervention pushes the system away, not toward, a market outcome, with considerable distributive consequences. US inaction would accept both these economic distortions and a unilateral choice on the part of Chinese authorities that has far-reaching consequences for the system as a whole. The ideal, first-best response would be for Chinese authorities to scale back their intervention. As of this writing, the IMF and Treasury Department have not achieved this result; although the renminbi has been allowed to appreciate against the dollar, the scale of intervention also increased substantially during 2007 compared with earlier years. Congress thus considers trade measures as a second-best remedy by default, not as the ideal solution. Trade measures that compensate for the distortion can in principle enhance *both* economic efficiency and fairness in international trade.

When implementing any such measures, however, several qualifications would be in order. Trade measures designed to counteract distortions created by currency manipulation should be (1) proportionate to the effect of the manipulation, as best as we can estimate it, (2) removed when manipulation ceases, and (3) removed if found to be irreconcilably inconsistent with US obligations in the WTO. Moreover, such countermeasures should not be applied in simple cases of undervaluation alone, but only in cases of undervaluation caused or perpetuated by manipulation. Even in the absence of manipulation, foreign exchange markets frequently undervalue and overvalue exchange rates, sometimes for prolonged periods. Selective, corrective intervention, cooperatively organized, is the better remedy for market-induced misalignments. Trade countermeasures should be reserved for cases of manipulation-induced undervaluation when the manipulator refuses to desist and when the economic consequences for the United States and international community are substantial. Such cases are rare, perhaps very rare, but the United States and the international system should have a robust capacity to counter such policy behavior and thus to discourage it in advance.

Reinforcing the IMF

The manipulation sections in the 1988 Act and in the IMF Articles of Agreement are important to the proper functioning and legitimate governance of the international economic system as a whole. Limitations on currency manipulation help to maintain widespread acceptance of that system as fair to the participants in globalization. Most international institutions such as the IMF, however, have difficulty enforcing hard rules by themselves, because, among other reasons, they often entrust enforcement to bodies in which the targets themselves and potential targets are members.

When hard rules are effective in the international realm, they are often supported by national measures. In the United Nations, Security Council decisions are enforced by national military units placed at the disposal of the United Nations for a specific contingency. In the WTO, dispute settlement decisions are given force largely by authorized retaliation on the part of the contracting parties. In the IMF, however, no national instruments are specifically provided for reinforcing the rules of the institution and the decisions of its governing bodies. Its principal instruments to compel cooperation are denial of funding—which does not apply to a country accumulating massive foreign exchange reserves by undervaluing its currency—denial of voting rights, and, in extreme cases, expulsion from the organization. The June 2007 revision to the exchange rate policy guidelines took a step in the right direction by giving more emphasis to the importance of misalignment, but probably does not make these provisions more enforceable. Antimanipulation legislation in the United States should be deliberately designed to provide a monetary analog to national enforcement instruments at the disposal of other international institutions.[4]

---

4. Mattoo and Subramanian (2008) take a different approach, arguing that the WTO should instead take on a greater role in combating manipulation by adopting a new set of rules related to exchange rates and adjudicating them in the dispute settlement mechanism. Setting aside for the moment the question of whether such a set of rules could be negotiated, their approach and the approach of strengthening the IMF would both require strengthening in turn the national instruments to reinforce multilateral decisions against rule breakers.

The adoption of manipulation countermeasures could be roughly analogous to the United States' use of trade measures in the late 1980s. At that time, Congress also witnessed weaker enforcement of international trade rules and less countervailing action on the part of the administration than it would have preferred. In response, Congress passed "Super 301" and the administration pursued several cases under this provision in subsequent years. The provision was broadly condemned as unilateralist, which indeed it was. But it also arguably advanced liberalization in the target countries on a multilateral, nondiscriminatory basis. Critically, as part of the Uruguay Round agreements, the United States effectively traded off use of Super and Section 301 for an enhanced dispute settlement mechanism in the WTO—agreeing to use Section 301 to redress denial of rights under the GATT/WTO agreements only with a favorable dispute settlement ruling. The dispute settlement mechanism thus created is widely regarded as well functioning and has been accepted by the United States.[5]

Any prospective use by the United States of antidumping or countervailing duties to combat currency undervaluation would meet similar international objections as heavy-handed unilateralism. An appropriate US response to these objections would be to trade off these instruments for more robust enforcement of the rules on exchange rate policy in the IMF's Articles of Agreement. Strengthening the IMF in this way would also require shoring up domestic political support for the institution in its member states, which in turn would be facilitated in the case of the United States by effective enforcement of the injunction against currency manipulation (Henning 2007b). Although it would initially involve the use of trade measures, such an agreement would ultimately shift the system toward the first-best solution.

Reinforcing the IMF in this way would not mean that the United States could not act unless the Fund finds that a particular country has manipulated its currency. Although the IMF has several advantages as a forum in which to address currency questions, the United States does not and should not fully outsource this element of exchange rate policy to the Fund. The United States has retained and should continue to retain unilateral means of action for cases in which others' policies impair the effective functioning of the international monetary system or prevent balance of payments adjustment, but in which the IMF is unwilling or unable to act. In such cases, however, the United States should use unilateral instruments in ways that are consistent with the rules and principles of the Fund and US obligations under the Articles of Agreement. We hope that

---

5. For reviews of Section 301 and Super 301, the Uruguay Round bargain creating the Dispute Settlement Understanding, and subsequent jurisprudence, see Bayard and Elliott (1994); Bhala (2001, chapter 19); and Jackson, Davey, and Sykes (2002, chapter 7).

such circumstances will be rare, but the Fund's recent posture toward Chinese currency policy shows that they do arise.

Multilateral Fairness and Coordination

If US exchange rate legislation pursues narrow, mercantilistic interests, then it will neither deserve nor receive international support. US policy objectives under any amended version of the 1988 Act must be in the interest of the system as a whole. Fortunately, the enlightened interest of the United States and the interest of the system coincide, while not perfectly, at least substantially. US actions to combat manipulation under the Act should also be in the interest of the target as well as that of third countries—which is currently the case for China.[6] Jettisoning the focus on the bilateral trade balance with the United States in favor of countries' global current account balances, and shifting analytical focus from nominal bilateral to real effective exchange rates, would also be helpful in this regard. These changes will support the multilateral legitimacy of US actions under the legislation. Just as Treasury must use its Exchange Stabilization Fund in ways that are consistent with its obligations in the IMF, Treasury should also have a mandate to adopt an internationalist perspective in exchange rate policy more broadly.

Relatedly, Congress should retain and enhance the obligation in the 1988 Act (section 3003) to pursue international coordination.[7] This obligation is consistent with Anne-Marie Slaughter's (2004) general advocacy of mandates for domestic agencies to cooperate internationally, thereby creating dual mandates for bureaucracies that constitute transnational government networks. Treasury's mandate to coordinate in international monetary affairs should be pursued and reported more affirmatively in the future than it has been over most of the period since the 1988 Act (see also Bergsten and Henning 1996). Successful coordination of course requires willing partners.[8] But if a partner makes a serious offer as part of a coordination package to smooth current account adjustment, for example, Treasury should have to explain any decision to reject. Congress should

---

6. Lardy (2006), for example, argues that exchange rate appreciation would advance the stated goals of senior Chinese policymakers to move toward consumption-driven growth. See also Lardy (2005).

7. Updated treatments of international macroeconomic policy coordination include Meyer et al. (2002); Canzoneri, Cumby, and Diba (2005); and Truman (2004). The political economy of coordination is discussed, among other places, in Andrews, Henning, and Pauly (2002); Henning (2006); and Andrews (2008).

8. Naturally, foreign partners of the United States should introduce similar mandates as well.

oversee this provision, and foreign governments should know that Congress would review Treasury's decisions in light of this mandate.

Report Consolidation

The US Treasury and Federal Reserve produce multiple reports related to exchange rate policy, as noted above. These reports nonetheless collectively (1) downplay, to put it mildly, the burning policy issues of the day, (2) are overlapping, (3) leave gaps, (4) cover different periods, and (5) rarely contain cross references. Congressional oversight and public discourse on exchange rate policy would benefit from streamlining and consolidating these reports. They need not be combined into one, but this still leaves room for substantial consolidation. Moreover, Congress should discipline itself when reviewing information requirements. Rather than mandating separate reports, as was done after the Mexican and Asian financial crises, Congress should insist that Treasury treat new, salient problems in the existing reports.

Preparing reports, testimony, and answers to questions from Congress consumes substantial staff time on the part of the Treasury. Congress must be realistic about allocating resources to support accountability if the process is to work well; this cannot be an afterthought. Congress must also devote its own staff resources to follow up on reports and prepare hearings where the secretary and other officials testify. To the extent that Congress cares more about exchange rate policy than it did in the past, its own staff and budget should reflect the shift. Neither Treasury nor the committees of jurisdiction should have to take on greater responsibilities without additional resources.

Congressional Oversight

Congress has not always been diligent in its oversight of exchange rate policy. The institutional separation of the consideration of currency and trade matters in the committees responsible for banking and trade, respectively, is one reason for the lapses in follow-up. This division of labor contributed to the lag in congressional activism during the mid-1980s, for example, and complicates Congress's follow-up on the broad international economic policy and specific manipulation issues in Treasury's reports. Making the linkage between trade, finance, and exchange rates is essential to understanding and redressing manipulation. To address this problem, I. M. Destler and I (Destler and Henning 1989, 155–58) recommended that the banking committee invite representatives from the trade and budget panels to participate in oversight hearings on the reports. The committees did this in several instances, both during the early years of the reporting process and in recent hearings devoted to China—but not systematically. Congress should now regularize multicommittee participation in oversight of exchange rate and international monetary policies by inviting members of the trade and budget committees to hearings of the banking committee. Multicommittee participation would help to integrate financial, trade, and macroeconomic concerns in the oversight process, give greater continuity to oversight over time, and help to render oversight more proactive and less reactive. It would also help to resolve jurisdictional disputes over trade and currency matters among these committees.

7

Conclusion

Congress long ago wisely delegated authority over exchange rate policy to the Treasury in cooperation with the Federal Reserve. To develop and execute policy effectively, the United States needs a strong Treasury capable of operating with flexibility in the markets and with broad discretion to cooperate with foreign partners. Extensive delegation, however, carries a reciprocal obligation for transparency, reporting, and accountability. When the US economy was relatively closed to international trade and capital flows, these agencies could often make and execute exchange rate policy outside the spotlight of Congress and national politics. However, globalization has raised the economic and political stakes associated with the external value of the dollar. Openness of the US economy increases the magnitude of the effect of exchange rates on firms and workers, making currency politics more contentious and simultaneously highlighting the importance of accountability in this policy arena.

This study reviews the Treasury's reports to Congress on exchange rate policy—introduced by the Exchange Rates and International Economic Policy Coordination Act of 1988—and Congress's treatment of them. It finds that the accountability process has often not worked well in practice: the coverage of the reports was sometimes incomplete and did not provide a sufficient basis for congressional oversight. Nor has Congress always performed its own role well, holding hearings on less than half of the reports and overlooking important substantive issues. Several recommendations can improve guidance to the Treasury, standards for assessment, and congressional oversight. These include (1) refining the criteria used to determine currency manipulation and writing them into law, (2) supporting the International Monetary Fund's enforcement of its rules on exchange rate policies, (3) clarifying the general objectives of US exchange rate policy, (4) reaffirming the mandate to seek international macroeconomic and currency cooperation, and (5) regularizing multi-committee oversight of exchange rate policy by Congress. Although several recent legislative proposals are motivated by the undervaluation of the Chinese currency, it is important to emphasize the broader purposes of the 1988 Act relating to the overall value of the dollar, its impact on the US economy, and international monetary stability. Any future legislation in this area should reinforce these broader purposes in addition to targeting currency manipulation.

Oversight and accountability of US exchange rate policy is important for reasons that transcend the economic health of the traded goods sector in the United States. Currency manipulation undercuts political support for the international monetary regime and globalization more broadly. By combating currency manipulation and prompting executive decision makers to consider the broad range of economic issues when setting policy with respect to the dollar, the authors of the 1988 Act sought to improve the functioning of the overall international monetary system and the perceived fairness with which that system operates. Anchoring policy more firmly in an effective accountability process would contribute to fairness in the globalization process and to sustaining broad political support for economic liberalization.

Globalization places stress on established institutions of democratic governance within countries. An increasing body of scholarship has been devoted to the impact of international economic integration on the democratic process in advanced, emerging, and developing countries, including the impact on mechanisms of accountability. Among other things, globalization can remove policy action from the reach of legislatures, introducing third parties, and reduce transparency. Confrontation in the United States over Chinese exchange rate policy provides a good example of the impact of the growing importance of the world economy and foreign governments for the evolving relationship between the Congress and executive branch. Failure to address shortcomings in accountability in this policy area could eventually present citizens with a choice between democratic control and economic openness. Strengthening the accountability mechanism, on the other hand, could help make globalization more consistent with democratic governance.

APPENDICES

Appendix A
Exchange Rates and International Economic Policy Coordination Act of 1988

Omnibus Trade and Competitiveness Act of 1988

Omnibus Trade and Competitiveness Act of 1988

TITLE III
International Financial Policy

Subtitle A
Exchange Rates and International Economic
Policy Coordination

Section 3001. Short Title

This subtitle may be cited as the "Exchange Rates and International Economic Policy Coordination Act of 1988."

Section 3002. Findings

The Congress finds that

(1) the macroeconomic policies, including the exchange rate policies, of the leading industrial nations require improved coordination and are not consistent with long-term economic growth and financial stability;

(2) currency values have a major role in determining the patterns of production and trade in the world economy;

(3) the rise in the value of the dollar in the early 1980s contributed substantially to our current trade deficit;

(4) exchange rates among major trading nations have become increasingly volatile and a pattern of exchange rates has at times developed which contributes to substantial and persistent imbalances in the flow of goods and services between nations, imposing serious strains on the world trading system and frustrating both business and government planning;

(5) capital flows between nations have become very large compared to trade flows, respond at times quickly and dramatically to economic and policy changes, and, for these reasons, contribute significantly to uncertainty in financial markets, the volatility of exchange rates, and the development of exchange rates which produce imbalances in the flow of goods and services between nations;

(6) policy initiatives between some trading nations that manipulate the value of their currencies in relation to the United States dollar to gain competitive advantage continue to create serious competitive problems for United States industries;

(7) a more stable exchange rate for the dollar at a level consistent with a more appropriate and sustainable level balance in the United States current account should be a major focus of national economic policy;

(8) procedures for improving the coordination of macroeconomic policy need to be strengthened considerably; and

(9) under appropriate circumstances, intervention by the United States in foreign exchange markets as part of coordinated international strategic intervention effort could produce more orderly adjustment of foreign exchange markets and, in combination with necessary macroeconomic policy changes, assist adjustment toward a more appropriate and sustainable balance in current accounts.

SECTION 3003. STATEMENT OF POLICY

It is the policy of the United States that

(1) the United States and the other major industrialized countries should take steps to continue the process of coordinating monetary, fiscal, and structural policies initiated in the Plaza Agreement of September 1985;

(2) the goal of the United States in international economic negotiations should be to achieve macroeconomic policies and exchange rates consistent with more appropriate and sustainable balances in trade and

capital flows and to foster price stability in conjunction with economic growth;

(3) the United States, in close coordination with the other major industrialized countries, should, where appropriate, participate in international currency markets with the objective of producing more orderly adjustment of foreign exchange markets and, in combination with necessary macroeconomic policy changes, assisting adjustment toward a more appropriate and sustainable balance in current accounts; and

(4) the accountability of the President for the impact of economic policies and exchange rates on trade competitiveness should be increased.

SECTION 3004. INTERNATIONAL NEGOTIATIONS ON EXCHANGE RATE AND ECONOMIC POLICIES

(a) MULTILATERAL NEGOTIATIONS—The President shall seek to confer and negotiate with other countries

(1) to achieve

(A) better coordination of macroeconomic policies of the major industrialized nations; and

(B) more appropriate and sustainable levels of trade and current account balances, and exchange rates of the dollar and other currencies consistent with such balances; and

(2) to develop a program for improving existing mechanisms for coordination and improving the functioning of the exchange rate system to provide for long-term exchange rate stability consistent with more appropriate and sustainable current account balances.

(b) BILATERAL NEGOTIATIONS—The Secretary of the Treasury shall analyze on an annual basis the exchange rate policies of foreign countries, in consultation with the International Monetary Fund, and consider whether countries manipulate the rate of exchange between their currency and the United States dollar for purposes of preventing effective balance of payments adjustments or gaining unfair competitive advantage in international trade. If the Secretary considers that such manipulation is occurring with respect to countries that (1) have material global current account surpluses; and (2) have significant bilateral trade surpluses with the United States, the Secretary of the Treasury shall take action to initiate negotiations with such foreign countries on an expedited basis, in the International Monetary Fund or bilaterally, for the purpose of ensuring that such countries regularly and promptly adjust the rate of exchange between their currencies and the United States dollar to permit effective balance of payments adjustments and to eliminate the unfair advantage. The Secretary shall not be required to initiate negotiations in cases where such negotiations would have a serious detrimental impact on vital national economic and security interests; in such cases, the Secretary shall inform the chairman and the ranking minority member of the Committee on Banking, Housing, and Urban Affairs of the Senate and of the Committee on Banking, Finance and Urban Affairs of the House of Representatives of his determination.

SECTION 3005. REPORTING REQUIREMENTS

(a) REPORTS REQUIRED—In furtherance of the purpose of this title, the Secretary, after consultation with the Chairman of the Board, shall submit to the Committee on Banking, Finance and Urban Affairs of the House of Representatives and the Committee on Banking, Housing, and Urban Affairs of the Senate, on or before October 15 each year, a written report on international economic policy, including exchange rate policy.

The Secretary shall provide a written update of developments six months after the initial report. In addition, the Secretary shall appear, if requested, before both committees to provide testimony on these reports.

(b) CONTENTS OF REPORT—Each report submitted under subsection (a) shall contain

(1) an analysis of currency market developments and the relationship between the United States dollar and the currencies of our major trade competitors;

(2) an evaluation of the factors in the United States and other economies that underlie conditions in the currency markets, including developments in bilateral trade and capital flows;

(3) a description of currency intervention or other actions undertaken to adjust the actual exchange rate of the dollar;

(4) an assessment of the impact of the exchange rate of the United States dollar on

(A) the ability of the United States to maintain a more appropriate and sustainable balance in its current account and merchandise trade account;

(B) production, employment, and noninflationary growth in the United States;

(C) the international competitive performance of United States industries and the external indebtedness of the United States;

(5) recommendations for any changes necessary in United States economic policy to attain a more appropriate and sustainable balance in the current account;

(6) the results of negotiations conducted pursuant to section 3004;

(7) key issues in United States policies arising from the most recent consultation requested by the International Monetary Fund under article IV of the Fund's Articles of Agreement; and

(8) a report on the size and composition of international capital flows, and the factors contributing to such flows, including, where possible, an assessment of the impact of such flows on exchange rates and trade flows.

[(c) REPORT BY BOARD OF GOVERNORS. Section 2A(1) of the Federal Reserve Act (12 U.S.C. 225a(1)) is amended by inserting after "the Nation" the following: ", including an analysis of the impact of the exchange rate of the dollar on those trends".]*

SECTION 3006. DEFINITIONS

As used in this subtitle:

(1) SECRETARY—The term "Secretary" means the Secretary of the Treasury.

(2) BOARD—The term "Board" means the Board of Governors of the Federal Reserve System.

---

* Bracketed section has since been removed from the law.

Appendix B
Articles of Agreement of the International Monetary Fund

ARTICLE IV

OBLIGATIONS REGARDING EXCHANGE ARRANGEMENTS

SECTION 1. GENERAL OBLIGATIONS OF MEMBERS

Recognizing that the essential purpose of the international monetary system is to provide a framework that facilitates the exchange of goods, services, and capital among countries, and that sustains sound economic growth, and that a principal objective is the continuing development of the orderly underlying conditions that are necessary for financial and economic stability, each member undertakes to collaborate with the Fund and other members to assure orderly exchange arrangements and to promote a stable system of exchange rates. In particular, each member shall:

(i) endeavor to direct its economic and financial policies toward the objective of fostering orderly economic growth with reasonable price stability, with due regard to its circumstances;

(ii) seek to promote stability by fostering orderly underlying economic and financial conditions and a monetary system that does not tend to produce erratic disruptions;

(iii) avoid manipulating exchange rates or the international monetary system in order to prevent effective balance of payments adjustment or to gain an unfair competitive advantage over other members; and

(iv) follow exchange policies compatible with the undertakings under this Section.

Section 3. Surveillance over Exchange Arrangements

(a) The Fund shall oversee the international monetary system in order to ensure its effective operation, and shall oversee the compliance of each member with its obligations under Section 1 of this Article.

(b) In order to fulfill its functions under (a) above, the Fund shall exercise firm surveillance over the exchange rate policies of members, and shall adopt specific principles for the guidance of all members with respect to those policies. Each member shall provide the Fund with the information necessary for such surveillance, and, when requested by the Fund, shall consult with it on the member's exchange rate policies. . . .

Appendix C
IMF Guidelines for Bilateral Surveillance over Members' Exchange Rate Policy

Excerpts from Executive Board Decision no. 5392-(77/63), April 29, 1977, as amended through June 15, 2007.

PART II. PRINCIPLES FOR THE GUIDANCE OF MEMBERS' POLICIES UNDER ARTICLE IV, SECTION 1

13. Principles A through D set out below are adopted pursuant to Article IV, Section 3(b) and are intended to provide guidance to members in the conduct of their exchange rate policies in accordance with their obligations under Article IV, Section 1. In accordance with Article IV, Section 3(b), these Principles are designed to respect the domestic social and political policies of members. In applying these principles, the Fund will pay due regard to the circumstances of members and, when determining whether a member is following these principles, the Fund will give the member the benefit of any reasonable doubt.

14. Principle A sets forth the obligation contained in Article IV, Section 1(iii); further guidance on its meaning is provided in the Annex to this Decision. Principles B through D constitute recommendations rather than obligations of members. A determination by the Fund that a member is not following one of these recommendations would not create a presumption that that member was in breach of its obligations under Article IV, Section 1.

A. A member shall avoid manipulating exchange rates or the international monetary system in order to prevent effective balance of payments adjustment or to gain an unfair competitive advantage over other members.

B. A member should intervene in the exchange market if necessary to counter disorderly conditions, which may be characterized *inter alia* by disruptive short-term movements in the exchange value of its currency.

C. Members should take into account in their intervention policies the interests of other members, including those of the countries in whose currencies they intervene.

D. A member should avoid exchange rate policies that are pursued for domestic reasons and result in external instability, including fundamental exchange rate misalignment.

15. In its surveillance of the observance by members of the principles set forth above, the Fund shall consider the following developments as among those which would require thorough review and might indicate the need for discussion with a member:

(i) protracted large-scale intervention in one direction in the exchange market, particularly if accompanied by sterilization;

(ii) official or quasi-official borrowing that either is unsustainable or brings unduly high liquidity risks, or excessive and prolonged official or quasi-official accumulation of foreign assets, for balance of payments purposes;

(iii) (a) the introduction, substantial intensification, or prolonged maintenance, for balance of payments purposes, of restrictions on, or incentives for, current transactions or payments, or

(b) the introduction or substantial modification for balance of payments purposes of restrictions on, or incentives for, the inflow or outflow of capital;

(iv) the pursuit, for balance of payments purposes, of monetary and other financial policies that provide abnormal encouragement or discouragement to capital flows;

(v) fundamental exchange rate misalignment;

(vi) large and prolonged current account deficits or surpluses; and

(vii) large external sector vulnerabilities, including liquidity risks, arising from private capital flows.

References

Aberbach, Joel D. 1990. *Keeping a Watchful Eye: The Politics of Congressional Oversight.* Washington: Brookings Institution.

Aberbach, Joel D. 2002. What's Happened to the Watchful Eye? *Congress and the Presidency* 29, no. 1 (Spring): 3–23.

Andrews, David M., ed. 2008. *Orderly Change: International Monetary Relations since Bretton Woods.* Ithaca and London: Cornell University Press.

Andrews, David M., C. Randall Henning, and Louis W. Pauly, eds. 2002. *Governing the World's Money.* Ithaca, NY: Cornell University Press.

Balassa, Bela, and John Williamson. 1987. *Adjusting to Success: Balance of Payments Policy in the East Asian NICs.* POLICY ANALYSES IN INTERNATIONAL ECONOMICS 17. Washington: Institute for International Economics.

Balassa, Bela, and John Williamson. 1990. *Adjusting to Success: Balance of Payments Policy in the East Asian NICs—Revised.* POLICY ANALYSES IN INTERNATIONAL ECONOMICS 17. Washington: Institute for International Economics.

Bayard, Thomas O., and Kimberly A. Elliott. 1994. *Reciprocity and Retaliation in US Trade Policy.* Washington: Institute for International Economics.

Bergsten, C. Fred, and C. Randall Henning. 1996. *Global Economic Leadership and the Group of Seven.* Washington: Institute for International Economics.

Bhala, Raj. 2001. *International Trade Law: Theory and Practice,* 2d ed. New York: Lexis Publishing.

Canzoneri, Matthew B., Robert E. Cumby, and Behzad T. Diba. 2005. The Need for International Policy Coordination: What's Old, What's New, What's Yet to Come? *Journal of International Economics* 66, no. 2 (July): 363–84.

Catte, Pietro, Giampaolo Galli, and Salvatore Rebecchini. 1994. Concerted Interventions and the Dollar: An Analysis of Daily Data. In *The International Monetary System,* eds. Peter B. Kenen, Francesco Papadia, and Fabrizio Saccomanni. Cambridge, UK: Cambridge University Press.

Cohen, Benjamin J. 2004. *The Future of Money.* Princeton: Princeton University Press.

de Grauwe, Paul, and Marianna Grimaldi. 2006. *The Exchange Rate in a Behavioral Finance Framework.* Princeton, NJ: Princeton University Press.

Destler, I. M. 2005. *American Trade Politics*, 4th ed. Washington: Institute for International Economics.

Destler, I. M. 2007. *American Trade Politics in 2007: Building Bipartisan Compromise.* Policy Briefs in International Economics 07-5. Washington: Peterson Institute for International Economics.

Destler, I. M., and C. Randall Henning. 1989. *Dollar Politics: Exchange Rate Policymaking in the United States.* Washington: Institute for International Economics.

Dominguez, Kathryn M., and Jeffrey A. Frankel. 1993. *Does Foreign Exchange Intervention Work?* Washington: Institute for International Economics.

Dooley, Michael P., David Folkerts-Landau, and Peter Garber. 2003. *An Essay on the Revived Bretton Woods System.* NBER Working Paper 9971 (September). Cambridge, MA: National Bureau of Economic Research.

Eichengreen, Barry J. 2004. *Global Imbalances and the Lessons of Bretton Woods.* NBER Working Paper 10497 (May). Cambridge, MA: National Bureau of Economic Research.

Epstein, David, and Sharyn O'Halloran. 1994. Administrative Procedures, Information, and Agency Discretion. *American Journal of Political Science* 38, no. 3 (August): 697–722.

Epstein, David, and Sharyn O'Halloran. 1995. A Theory of Strategic Oversight: Congress, Lobbyists, and the Bureaucracy. *Journal of Law, Economics and Organization*, no. 11: 227–55.

Epstein, David, and Sharyn O'Halloran. 1999. *Delegating Powers: A Transaction Cost Politics Approach to Policy Making under Separate Powers.* New York: Cambridge University Press.

Evans, Peter B., Harold K. Jacobson, and Robert D. Putnam. 1993. *Double-Edged Diplomacy: International Bargaining and Domestic Politics.* Studies in International Political Economy 25. Berkeley: University of California Press.

Fatum, Rasmus, and Michael M. Hutchison. 2005. Foreign Exchange Intervention and Monetary Policy in Japan, 2003–2004. *International Economics and Economic Policy*, no. 2: 241–60.

Frankel, Jeffrey A. 1992. Foreign Exchange Policy, Monetary Policy and Capital Market Liberalization in Korea. Paper presented at the US-Korea Academic Symposium III: Korean-US Financial Issues, Korea Economic Institute, Columbia University, New York, September 2–3.

Frankel, Jeffrey A. 1995. Exchange Rate Policy. In *American Economic Policy in the 1980s*, ed. Martin Feldstein. Chicago: University of Chicago Press.

Frankel, Jeffrey A., and Shang-Jin Wei. 2007. *Assessing China's Exchange Rate Regime.* NBER Working Paper 13100 (May). Cambridge, MA: National Bureau of Economic Research.

Fratzscher, Marcel. 2004. *Communication and Exchange Rate Policy.* ECB Working Paper 363. Frankfurt: European Central Bank.

Funabashi, Y. 1988. *Managing the Dollar: From the Plaza to the Louvre.* Washington: Institute for International Economics.

GAO (General Accounting Office). 1989. *U.S. Trade Deficit* (April). Washington: US Government Printing Office.

GAO (Government Accountability Office). 2005. *International Trade: Treasury Assessments Have Not Found Currency Manipulation, but Concerns about Exchange Rates Continue.* Report to Congressional Committees (April). Washington.

Genberg, Hans, and Alexander Swoboda. 2005. Exchange-Rate Regimes: Does What Countries Say Matter? *IMF Staff Papers* 52, Special Issue: 129–41.

Goldstein, Morris. 1997. *The Asian Financial Crisis: Causes, Cures, and Systemic Implications.* POLICY ANALYSES IN INTERNATIONAL ECONOMICS 55. Washington: Institute for International Economics.

Goldstein, Morris. 2004. *Adjusting China's Exchange Rate Policies.* Working Paper 04-1. Washington: Institute for International Economics.

Goldstein, Morris. 2005. Renminbi Controversies. Paper presented at a conference on monetary institutions and economic development, Cato Institute, Washington, November 3.

Goldstein, Morris. 2006. Currency Manipulation and Enforcing the Rules of the International Monetary System. In *Reforming the IMF for the 21st Century*, ed. Edwin M. Truman. Washington: Institute for International Economics.

Goldstein, Morris. 2007. *A (Lack of) Progress Report on China's Exchange Rate Policies*. Working Paper 07-5. Washington: Peterson Institute for International Economics.

Goldstein, Morris, and Nicholas R. Lardy. 2005. *China's Role in the Revived Bretton Woods System: A Case of Mistaken Identity*. Working Paper 05-2. Washington: Institute for International Economics.

Goldstein, Morris, and Nicholas R. Lardy, eds. 2008. *Debating China's Exchange Rate Policy*. Washington: Peterson Institute for International Economics.

Grant, Ruth W., and Robert O. Keohane. 2005. Accountability and Abuses of Power in World Politics. *American Political Science Review* 99, no. 1 (February): 29–44.

Havrilesky, Thomas M. 1995. *The Pressures on American Monetary Policy*, 2d ed. Boston, MA: Kluwer Academic Publishers

Helleiner, Eric, and Jonathan Kirshner, eds. 2008. *At Home Abroad? The Dollar's Destiny as a World Currency*. Special section of *Review of International Political Economy* (vol. 15, no. 3, forthcoming).

Henning, C. Randall. 1994. *Currencies and Politics in the United States, Germany, and Japan*. Washington: Institute for International Economics.

Henning, C. Randall. 1997. *Cooperating with Europe's Monetary Union*. POLICY ANALYSES IN INTERNATIONAL ECONOMICS 49. Washington: Institute for International Economics.

Henning, C. Randall. 1999. *The Exchange Stabilization Fund: Slush Money or War Chest?* POLICY ANALYSES IN INTERNATIONAL ECONOMICS 57. Washington: Institute for International Economics.

Henning, C. Randall. 2000. US-EU Relations after the Inception of the Monetary Union: Cooperation or Rivalry? In *Transatlantic Perspectives on the Euro*, eds. C. Randall Henning and Pier Carlo Padoan. Washington: European Community Studies Association and Brookings Institution.

Henning, C. Randall. 2006. *The External Policy of the Euro Area: Organizing for Foreign Exchange Intervention*. Working Paper 06-4 (June). Washington: Institute for International Economics.

Henning, C. Randall. 2007a. Democratic Accountability and the Exchange Rate Policy of the Euro Area. *Review of International Political Economy* 14, no. 5 (December): 774–99.

Henning, C. Randall. 2007b. Institutional Strategy for the Global Economy. In *C. Fred Bergsten and the World Economy*, ed. Michael Mussa. Washington: Peterson Institute for International Economics.

Hufbauer, Gary Clyde, Yee Wong, and Ketki Sheth. 2006. *US-China Trade Disputes: Rising Tide, Rising Stake*. POLICY ANALYSES IN INTERNATIONAL ECONOMICS 78. Washington: Institute for International Economics.

Hufbauer, Gary Clyde, and Claire Brunel. 2008. The US Congress and the Chinese Renminbi. In *Debating China's Exchange Rate Policy*, eds. Morris Goldstein and Nicholas R. Lardy. Washington: Peterson Institute for International Economics.

IMF (International Monetary Fund). 2006. Article IV of the Fund's Articles of Agreement: An Overview of the Legal Framework. Washington: IMF Legal Department.

IMF (International Monetary Fund). 2007. Principles for the Guidance of Members' Policies under Article IV, Section 1. Executive Board Decision no. 5392-(77/63), April 29, 1977, as amended through June 15, 2007. Washington.

Ito, Takatoshi. 2002. *Is Foreign Exchange Intervention Effective? The Japanese Experiences in the 1990s*. NBER Working Paper 8914. Cambridge, MA: National Bureau of Economic Research.

Jackson, John H., William J. Davey, and Alan O. Sykes, Jr. 2002. *Legal Problems of International Economics Relations: Cases, Materials and Text*, 4th ed. St. Paul, MN: West Group.

Kim, Kihwan. 1993. The Political Economy of U.S.-Korea Trade Friction in the 1980s: A Korean Perspective. In *Shaping a New Economic Relationship: The Republic of Korea and the United States*, eds. Jongryn Mo and Ramon H. Myers. Stanford, CA: Hoover Press.

Kubelec, Christopher. 2004. Intervention When Misalignments Are Large. In *Dollar Adjustment: How Far? Against What?* Special Report 17, eds. C. Fred Bergsten and John Williamson. Washington: Institute for International Economics.

Lardy, Nicholas R. 1994. *China in the World Economy*. Washington: Institute for International Economics.

Lardy, Nicholas R. 2005. China: The Great New Economic Challenge? In *The United States in the World Economy: Foreign Economic Policy for the Next Decade*, C. Fred Bergsten and the Institute for International Economics. Washington: Institute for International Economics.

Lardy, Nicholas R. 2006. *China: Toward a Consumption-Driven Growth Path*. Policy Briefs in International Economics 06-6. Washington: Peterson Institute for International Economics.

Mann, Catherine L. 1999. *Is the U.S. Trade Deficit Sustainable?* Washington: Institute for International Economics.

Mann, Thomas E., and Norman J. Ornstein. 2006. *The Broken Branch: How Congress is Failing America and How to Get It Back on Track*. Oxford and New York: Oxford University Press.

Masson, Paul R., Thomas H. Krueger, and Bart G. Turtelboom. 1997. *EMU and the International Monetary System*. Washington: International Monetary Fund.

Mattoo, Aaditya, and Arvind Subramanian. 2008. *Currency Undervaluation and Sovereign Wealth Funds: A New Role for the World Trade Organization*. Working Paper 08-2. Washington: Peterson Institute for International Economics.

McCowan, T. Ashby, Patricia Pollard, and John Weeks. 2007. *Equilibrium Exchange Rate Models and Misalignments*. Office of International Affairs Occasional Paper 7 (March). Washington: Department of the Treasury.

McCubbins, Mathew, Roger Noll, and Barry Weingast. 1987. Administrative Procedures as Instruments of Political Control. *Journal of Law, Economics and Organization*, no. 3: 243–77.

McCubbins, Mathew, Roger Noll, and Barry Weingast. 1989. Structure and Process, Politics and Policy: Administrative Arrangements and the Political Control of Agencies. *Virginia Law Review*, no. 75: 431–82.

McCubbins, Mathew, and Thomas Schwartz. 1984. Congressional Oversight Overlooked: Police Patrols versus Fire Alarms. *American Journal of Political Science*, no. 2: 165–79.

McKinnon, Ronald. 2006. *Exchange Rates under the East Asian Dollar Standard*. Cambridge, MA and London: MIT Press.

Meyer, Laurence H., Brian M. Doyle, Joseph E. Gagnon, and Dale W. Henderson. 2002. *International Coordination of Macroeconomic Policies: Still Alive in the New Millennium?* International Finance Discussion Papers 723. Washington: Board of Governors of the Federal Reserve System.

Mo, Jongryn, and Ramon H. Myers, eds. 1993. *Shaping a New Economic Relationship: The Republic of Korea and the United States*. Stanford, CA: Hoover Press.

Morris, Irvin L. 2000. *Congress, the President, and the Federal Reserve: The Politics of American Monetary Policy-making*. Ann Arbor, MI: University of Michigan Press.

Mullen, Patrick R. 2006. Congressional Reporting: A Management Process to Build a Legislative-Centered Public Administration. Doctoral dissertation, Virginia Tech University.

Mussa, Michael. 2007. IMF Surveillance over China's Exchange Rate Policy. Paper presented at a conference on China's exchange rate policy, Peterson Institute for International Economics, Washington, October 19.

Noland, Marcus. 1997. Chasing Phantoms: The Political Economy of USTR. *International Organization*, no. 51: 365–87.

People's Bank of China. 2005. *China Monetary Policy Report, Quarter Two*. Beijing.

Putnam, Robert D. 1988. Diplomacy and Domestic Politics: The Logic of Two-Level Games. *International Organization*, no. 42 (Summer): 427–60.

Ramaswamy, Ramana, and Hossein Samiei. 2003. The Yen-Dollar Rate: Have Interventions Mattered? In *Japan's Lost Decade: Policies for Economic Revival*, eds. Tim Callen and Jonathan D. Ostry. Washington: International Monetary Fund.

Rosenbloom, David H. 2000. *Building a Legislative-Centered Public Administration: Congress and the Administrative State, 1946–1999*. Tuscaloosa, AL: The University of Alabama Press.

Rubin, Robert E., and Jacob Weisberg. 2003. *In an Uncertain World: Tough Choices from Wall Street to Washington*. New York: Random House.

Sarno, Lucio, and Mark P. Taylor. 2001. Official Intervention in the Foreign Exchange Market: Is It Effective and, If So, How Does It Work? *Journal of Economic Literature* 39, no. 3: 839–68.

Schelling, Thomas C. 1960. *The Strategy of Conflict*. Cambridge, MA: Harvard University Press.

Shepsle, Kenneth. 1992. Bureaucratic Drift, Coalition Drift and Time Consistency: A Comment on Macey. *Journal of Law, Economics, and Organization*, no. 8: 111–18.

Slaughter, Anne-Marie. 2004. *A New World Order*. Princeton, NJ: Princeton University Press.

Sobel, Mark, and Louellen Stedman. 2006. *The Evolution of the G-7 and Economic Policy Coordination*. Office of International Affairs Occasional Paper no. 3 (July). Washington: Department of the Treasury.

Taylor, John B. 2007. *Global Financial Warriors: The Untold Story of International Finance in the Post-9/11 World*. New York: W. W. Norton.

Taylor, Mark. 2003. *Is Official Exchange Rate Intervention Effective?* CEPR Discussion Paper no. 3758. London: Centre for Economic Policy Research.

Truman, Edwin M. 2004. A Critical Review of Coordination Efforts in the Past. In *Macroeconomic Policies in the World Economy*, ed. Horst Siebert. Berlin: Springer-Verlag.

US Congress. 1988. Omnibus Trade and Competitiveness Act of 1988. Conference report to accompany HR 3, 100th Congress, 2nd session, Report 100-576, April 20. Washington: US Government Printing Office.

US House of Representatives, Committee on Banking, Finance and Urban Affairs. 1987. Title IV of the Trade and International Economic Policy Reform Act of 1987. Report to accompany HR 3, 100th Congress, 1st session, April 6. Washington: US Government Printing Office.

US House of Representatives, Joint Economic Committee. 1995. Hearing on The Humphrey-Hawkins Act and the Role of the Federal Reserve, 104th Congress, 2nd session, Washington, March 16.

US House of Representatives, Committee on Banking and Financial Services. 1997. Hearing on the East Asian Economic Conditions Part I, 105th Congress, 1st session, Washington, November 17.

US House of Representatives, Committee on Banking and Financial Services. 1998a. Hearing on the East Asian Economic Conditions Part II, 105th Congress, 2nd session, Washington, January 30 and February 3.

US House of Representatives, Committee on Banking and Financial Services. 1998b. Hearing on the European Monetary Union. 105th Congress, 2nd session, Washington, April 28.

US House of Representatives, Office of the Clerk. 2007. Reports to be made to Congress. Washington: US Government Printing Office.

US Senate, Committee on Banking, Housing, and Urban Affairs. 1987. United States Trade Enhancement Act of 1987. Report to accompany S 1409, 100th Congress, 1st session, June 23. Washington: US Government Printing Office.

US Senate, Finance Committee, Subcommittee on International Trade. 1989. Hearing on Currency Manipulation, 101st Congress, 1st session, Washington, May 12.

US Senate, Committee on Banking, Housing, and Urban Affairs. 1995. Hearing on the Mexican Peso Crisis, 104th Congress, 1st session, Washington, January 31, March 9–10, May 24, and July 14.

US Senate, Committee on Banking, Housing, and Urban Affairs, Subcommittee on International Trade and Finance. 1999. Hearing on Oversight on How the International Monetary Fund Is Implementing the Reforms Mandated Last Year in the Omnibus Appropriations Bill, 106th Congress, 1st session, Washington, March 9.

US Senate, Committee on Banking, Housing, and Urban Affairs. 2002. Hearing on the US Department of the Treasury's Report to Congress on International Economic and Exchange Rate Policy, 107th Congress, 2nd session, Washington, May 1.

US Senate, Committee on the Budget. 1997. Europe's Monetary Union and Its Potential Impact on the United States Economy, 105th Congress, 1st session. Washington: US Government Printing Office.

US Treasury. Various years. *Report to the Congress on International Economic and Exchange Rate Policy*. Washington.

US Treasury. 1995a. *Treasury Secretary's Report to Congress*. Report pursuant to the Mexican Debt Disclosure Act of 1995 (May). Washington.

US Treasury. 1995b. *Semi-Annual Report to Congress by the Secretary of the Treasury on Behalf of the President*. Report pursuant to the Mexican Debt Disclosure Act of 1995 (June 30). Washington.

US Treasury. 1996. *Treasury Secretary's Mexico Report*. Report pursuant to the Mexican Debt Disclosure Act of 1995 (December). Washington.

US Treasury. 2005. *Report to the Committees on Appropriations on Clarifications of Statutory Provisions Addressing Currency Manipulation* (March 11). Washington.

Wang, Yen-Kyun. 1993. Exchange Rates, Current Account Balance of Korea, and U.S. Korea Negotiations on Exchange-Rate Policy. In *Shaping a New Economic Relationship: The Republic of Korea and the United States*, eds. Jongryn Mo and Ramon H. Myers. Stanford, CA: Hoover Press.

Williamson, John. 1998. Crawling Bands or Monitoring Bands: How to Manage Exchange Rates in a World of Capital Mobility. *International Finance*, no. 1: 59–79.

Williamson, John. 2000. *Exchange Rate Regimes for Emerging Markets: Reviving the Intermediate Option*. POLICY ANALYSES IN INTERNATIONAL ECONOMICS 60. Washington: Institute for International Economics.

Williamson, John. 2007. *Reference Rates and the International Monetary System*. POLICY ANALYSES IN INTERNATIONAL ECONOMICS 82. Washington: Peterson Institute for International Economics.

Woolley, John T. 1984. *Monetary Politics: The Federal Reserve and the Politics of Monetary Policy*. New York: Cambridge University Press.

Index

accountability, 2, 11–16
  assessment of, 52–55, 85, 87–88, 99–100
  currency manipulation and, 47, 49–50
  definition of, 11
  delegation and, 15–16
  dysfunctionalities in, 15–16
  of executive, 20, 40
  international comparison of, 7
  prerequisites for, 11–13
  role of Congress in, 14–16, 67–68
  transparency and, 12–13, 86
antidumping duties, 92, 94
Asian financial crisis (1997–98), 15n, 36–37, 44–45, 86
Asian newly industrialized countries. *See* newly industrialized countries; *specific country*

Bentsen, Lloyd, 35n, 37, 41
Bernanke, Ben S., 54–55, 55n
bilateral trade balance
  currency manipulation decisions and, 34, 88–89
  mandated negotiations and, 20, 22, 48, 87–89
borrowing, foreign, 42–43
Brady, Nicholas F., 34, 40, 43, 43n, 66
Bretton Woods regime, 12
budget deficits, 39–42, 86, 88

Bush, George H. W. administration, 34, 40, 52
Bush, George W. administration, 41–42, 43, 45, 49, 50, 52–53, 66–67

capital mobility, 2
Case Act, 14
China. *See also* renminbi
  current account balance, 27, 31f, 46, 88
  exchange rate policy, 1, 3n, 3–4, 8, 100
    reform of, 45–46
    Treasury warnings about, 27, 27n, 29, 31, 33, 33n, 34, 37, 44–53, 66–67
  foreign exchange reserves, 44
  as scapegoat, 34
  Strategic Economic Dialogue with, 50–52, 51n
  trade liberalization, 31
  Treasury reports on, 44–52
  US trade balance with, 27, 33f
  WTO accession, 31
Clinton administration, 34–36, 35n, 37, 41, 52
competitiveness, currency manipulation and, 19, 91–92
Congress
  authority over exchange rate policy, 3, 11–12
  budget deficit analyses, 40n

investment, international, 42–43
Iraq, "Desert Storm" invasion of, 41n

Japanese yen
    Treasury reports on, 37–38
    US dollar exchange rate against, 25f, 37

Korea
    currency manipulation, 24, 24n, 26, 28f,
        34, 46, 48, 50
    current account balance, 24, 30f
    as scapegoat, 34
    US trade balance with, 26, 32f
Korean won, dollar exchange rate against,
    24, 28f

legislation, 18–19, 67, 77t–83t. *See also*
    specific act
Louvre Accord, 18

Maastricht Treaty, 39
macroeconomic policy, exchange rate
    policy and, 39–44, 86–88
Mexican Debt Disclosure Act of 1995, 36
Mexican peso crisis (1994–95), 15n,
    34–36, 86
monetary policy. *See* fiscal policy
Mulford, David C., 24, 34, 55, 66
multilateral coordination, 95–96
multilateral negotiations
    versus bilateral, 20, 88–89, 95–96
    countermeasures in context of, 92,
        94–95
    versus unilateral action, 94–95

national saving rate, 41–42
negotiations
    currency manipulation and, 51–52
    mandated, 20–22, 36, 48, 87–88
    multilateral versus bilateral, 20, 88–89,
        95–96
    three-part test for, 20–21
newly industrialized countries (NIEs).
    See also specific country
    currency manipulation by, 34, 46, 48, 50
    exchange rate equalization tariff, 18
    US trade balance with, 26, 32f–33f
North American Free Trade Agreement
    (NAFTA), 34

Office of International Affairs (Treasury),
    53
Office of Management and Budget
    (OMB), 40n

official statements, market sensitivity to, 5
Omnibus Trade and Competitiveness Act
    of 1988, 17, 18, 103
    Super 301 provision, 24, 31, 94, 94n
O'Neill, Paul, 45, 46, 48

Paulson, Henry M., Jr., 1, 48, 67
Plaza Accord, 18, 20, 24
political aspects
    of congressional oversight, 66
    of currency manipulation, 100
    of international economic policy, 2
    of Treasury reports, 53, 55
president. *See* executive; *specific president*
Proxmire, William, 43n, 66
public signals
    currency manipulation designation
        and, 51
    Treasury reports as tools for, 55

"rational expectations" view, 4
Reagan administration, 13, 17–18, 39, 67
Reagan-Volcker policy mix, 17
real effective exchange rates, 26f, 47, 48
    current account balance and, 88–89, 95
Regan, Donald T., 17, 18, 21
renminbi (Chinese)
    appreciation of, 46, 92
    dollar peg, 44–45
    undervaluation of, 1, 3, 46
    US dollar exchange rate against,
        29, 29f
reporting requirements, 14–15, 21–22, 96,
    106–107. *See also* Federal Reserve
    reports; Treasury reports
Rubin, Robert, 37, 41, 47

Sarbanes, Paul, 45, 66
saving rate, 41–42
scapegoating, 15, 34
Schumer, Charles, 48, 91
Smoot-Hawley bill, 18
Snow, John, 45, 47, 48
Strategic Economic Dialogue, 1, 48,
    50–52, 51n
Summers, Lawrence, 37, 41, 44, 45, 47
Super 301 provision, 24, 31, 94, 94n

Taiwan
    currency manipulation by, 24, 24n, 26,
        28f, 34, 46, 48, 50
    current account balance, 24, 30f
    as scapegoat, 34
    US trade balance with, 26, 32f

Other Publications from the Peterson Institute

The Future of World Trade in Textiles and Apparel* William R. Cline
1987, 2d ed. June *1999* ISBN 0-88132-110-9
Completing the Uruguay Round: A Results-Oriented Approach to the GATT Trade Negotiations* Jeffrey J. Schott, editor
September 1990 ISBN 0-88132-130-3
Economic Sanctions Reconsidered (2 volumes)
Economic Sanctions Reconsidered: Supplemental Case Histories
Gary Clyde Hufbauer, Jeffrey J. Schott, and Kimberly Ann Elliott
1985, 2d ed. Dec. 1990 ISBN cloth 0-88132-115-X
ISBN paper 0-88132-105-2
Economic Sanctions Reconsidered: History and Current Policy Gary Clyde Hufbauer, Jeffrey J. Schott, and Kimberly Ann Elliott
December 1990 ISBN cloth 0-88132-140-0
ISBN paper 0-88132-136-2
Pacific Basin Developing Countries: Prospects for Economic Sanctions Reconsidered: History and Current Policy Gary Clyde Hufbauer, Jeffrey J. Schott, and Kimberly Ann Elliott
December 1990 ISBN cloth 0-88132-140-0
ISBN paper 0-88132-136-2
Pacific Basin Developing Countries: Prospects for the Future* Marcus Noland
January 1991 ISBN cloth 0-88132-141-9
ISBN paper 0-88132-081-1
Currency Convertibility in Eastern Europe* John Williamson, editor
October 1991 ISBN 0-88132-128-1
International Adjustment and Financing: The Lessons of 1985-1991* C. Fred Bergsten, editor
January 1992 ISBN 0-88132-112-5
North American Free Trade: Issues and Recommendations*
Gary Clyde Hufbauer and Jeffrey J. Schott
April 1992 ISBN 0-88132-120-6
Narrowing the U.S. Current Account Deficit*
Alan J. Lenz/*June 1992* ISBN 0-88132-103-6
The Economics of Global Warming
William R. Cline/*June 1992* ISBN 0-88132-132-X
US Taxation of International Income: Blueprint for Reform Gary Clyde Hufbauer, assisted by Joanna M. van Rooij
October 1992 ISBN 0-88132-134-6
Who's Bashing Whom? Trade Conflict in High-Technology Industries
Laura D'Andrea Tyson
November 1992 ISBN 0-88132-106-0
Korea in the World Economy*
Il SaKong
January 1993 ISBN 0-88132-183-4
Pacific Dynamism and the International Economic System*
C. Fred Bergsten and Marcus Noland, editors
May 1993 ISBN 0-88132-196-6
Economic Consequences of Soviet Disintegration* John Williamson, editor
May 1993 ISBN 0-88132-190-7

Reconcilable Differences?
United States-Japan Economic Conflict*
C. Fred Bergsten and Marcus Noland
June 1993 ISBN 0-88132-129-X
Does Foreign Exchange Intervention Work?
Kathryn M. Dominguez and Jeffrey A. Frankel
September 1993 ISBN 0-88132-104-4
Sizing Up U.S. Export Disincentives*
J. David Richardson
September 1993 ISBN 0-88132-107-9
NAFTA: An Assessment Gary Clyde Hufbauer and Jeffrey J. Schott/*rev. ed.*
October 1993 ISBN 0-88132-199-0
Adjusting to Volatile Energy Prices
Philip K. Verleger, Jr.
November 1993 ISBN 0-88132-069-2
The Political Economy of Policy Reform
John Williamson, editor
January 1994 ISBN 0-88132-195-8
Measuring the Costs of Protection in the United States Gary Clyde Hufbauer and Kimberly Ann Elliott
January 1994 ISBN 0-88132-108-7
The Dynamics of Korean Economic Development* Cho Soon
March 1994 ISBN 0-88132-162-1
Reviving the European Union*
C. Randall Henning, Eduard Hochreiter, and Gary Clyde Hufbauer, editors
April 1994 ISBN 0-88132-208-3
China in the World Economy
Nicholas R. Lardy
April 1994 ISBN 0-88132-200-8
Greening the GATT: Trade, Environment, and the Future Daniel C. Esty
July 1994 ISBN 0-88132-205-9
Western Hemisphere Economic Integration*
Gary Clyde Hufbauer and Jeffrey J. Schott
July 1994 ISBN 0-88132-159-1
Currencies and Politics in the United States, Germany, and Japan C. Randall Henning
September 1994 ISBN 0-88132-127-3
Estimating Equilibrium Exchange Rates
John Williamson, editor
September 1994 ISBN 0-88132-076-5
Managing the World Economy: Fifty Years after Bretton Woods Peter B. Kenen, editor
September 1994 ISBN 0-88132-212-1
Reciprocity and Retaliation in U.S. Trade Policy
Thomas O. Bayard and Kimberly Ann Elliott
September 1994 ISBN 0-88132-084-6
The Uruguay Round: An Assessment*
Jeffrey J. Schott, assisted by Johanna W. Buurman
November 1994 ISBN 0-88132-206-7
Measuring the Costs of Protection in Japan*
Yoko Sazanami, Shujiro Urata, and Hiroki Kawai
January 1995 ISBN 0-88132-211-3

Foreign Direct Investment in the
United States, 3d ed.,
Edward M. Graham and Paul R. Krugman
January 1995   ISBN 0-88132-204-0
The Political Economy of Korea-United
States Cooperation*
C. Fred Bergsten and Il SaKong, editors
February 1995   ISBN 0-88132-213-X
International Debt Reexamined*
William R. Cline
February 1995   ISBN 0-88132-083-8
American Trade Politics, 3d ed.
I. M. Destler
April 1995   ISBN 0-88132-215-6
Managing Official Export Credits:
The Quest for a Global Regime*
John E. Ray
July 1995   ISBN 0-88132-207-5
Asia Pacific Fusion: Japan's Role in APEC*
Yoichi Funabashi
October 1995   ISBN 0-88132-224-5
Korea-United States Cooperation in the New
World Order* C. Fred Bergsten and Il SaKong, eds.
February 1996   ISBN 0-88132-226-1
Why Exports Really Matter!* ISBN 0-88132-221-0
Why Exports Matter More!* ISBN 0-88132-229-6
J. David Richardson and Karin Rindal
July 1995; February 1996
Global Corporations and National Governments
Edward M. Graham
May 1996   ISBN 0-88132-111-7
Global Economic Leadership and the Group of
Seven   C. Fred Bergsten and C. Randall Henning
May 1996   ISBN 0-88132-218-0
The Trading System after the Uruguay Round*
John Whalley and Colleen Hamilton
July 1996   ISBN 0-88132-131-1
Private Capital Flows to Emerging Markets
after the Mexican Crisis*
Guillermo A. Calvo, Morris Goldstein,
and Eduard Hochreiter
September 1996   ISBN 0-88132-232-6
The Crawling Band as an Exchange Rate Regime:
Lessons from Chile, Colombia, and Israel
John Williamson
September 1996   ISBN 0-88132-231-8
Flying High: Liberalizing Civil Aviation
in the Asia Pacific*
Gary Clyde Hufbauer and Christopher Findlay
November 1996   ISBN 0-88132-227-X
Measuring the Costs of Visible Protection
in Korea*   Namdoo Kim
November 1996   ISBN 0-88132-236-9
The World Trading System: Challenges Ahead
Jeffrey J. Schott
December 1996   ISBN 0-88132-235-0
Has Globalization Gone Too Far?
Dani Rodrik
March 1997   ISBN paper 0-88132-241-5

Korea-United States Economic Relationship*
C. Fred Bergsten and Il SaKong, editors
March 1997   ISBN 0-88132-240-7
Summitry in the Americas: A Progress Report
Richard E. Feinberg
April 1997   ISBN 0-88132-242-3
Corruption and the Global Economy
Kimberly Ann Elliott
June 1997   ISBN 0-88132-233-4
Regional Trading Blocs in the World
Economic System   Jeffrey A. Frankel
October 1997   ISBN 0-88132-202-4
Sustaining the Asia Pacific Miracle:
Environmental Protection and Economic
Integration   Andre Dua and Daniel C. Esty
October 1997   ISBN 0-88132-250-4
Trade and Income Distribution
William R. Cline
November 1997   ISBN 0-88132-216-4
Global Competition Policy
Edward M. Graham and J. David Richardson
December 1997   ISBN 0-88132-166-4
Unfinished Business: Telecommunications
after the Uruguay Round
Gary Clyde Hufbauer and Erika Wada
December 1997   ISBN 0-88132-257-1
Financial Services Liberalization in the WTO
Wendy Dobson and Pierre Jacquet
June 1998   ISBN 0-88132-254-7
Restoring Japan's Economic Growth
Adam S. Posen
September 1998   ISBN 0-88132-262-8
Measuring the Costs of Protection in China
Zhang Shuguang, Zhang Yansheng,
and Wan Zhongxin
November 1998   ISBN 0-88132-247-4
Foreign Direct Investment and Development:
The New Policy Agenda for Developing
Countries and Economies in Transition
Theodore H. Moran
December 1998   ISBN 0-88132-258-X
Behind the Open Door: Foreign Enterprises
in the Chinese Marketplace   Daniel H. Rosen
January 1999   ISBN 0-88132-263-6
Toward A New International Financial
Architecture: A Practical Post-Asia Agenda
Barry Eichengreen
February 1999   ISBN 0-88132-270-9
Is the U.S. Trade Deficit Sustainable?
Catherine L. Mann
September 1999   ISBN 0-88132-265-2
Safeguarding Prosperity in a Global Financial
System: The Future International Financial
Architecture, Independent Task Force Report
Sponsored by the Council on Foreign Relations
Morris Goldstein, Project Director
October 1999   ISBN 0-88132-287-3
Avoiding the Apocalypse: The Future
of the Two Koreas   Marcus Noland
June 2000   ISBN 0-88132-278-4

4 Global Economic Imbalances*
C. Fred Bergsten, editor
March 1986   ISBN 0-88132-042-0
5 African Debt and Financing*
Carol Lancaster and John Williamson, eds.
May 1986   ISBN 0-88132-044-7
6 Resolving the Global Economic Crisis:
After Wall Street*   by Thirty-three
Economists from Thirteen Countries
December 1987   ISBN 0-88132-070-6
7 World Economic Problems*
Kimberly Ann Elliott/John Williamson, eds.
April 1988   ISBN 0-88132-055-2
Reforming World Agricultural Trade*
by Twenty-nine Professionals from
Seventeen Countries
1988   ISBN 0-88132-088-9
8 Economic Relations Between the United
States and Korea: Conflict or Cooperation?*
Thomas O. Bayard and Soogil Young, eds.
January 1989   ISBN 0-88132-068-4
9 Whither APEC? The Progress to Date
and Agenda for the Future*
C. Fred Bergsten, editor
October 1997   ISBN 0-88132-248-2
10 Economic Integration of the Korean
Peninsula   Marcus Noland, editor
January 1998   ISBN 0-88132-255-5
11 Restarting Fast Track*   Jeffrey J. Schott, ed.
April 1998   ISBN 0-88132-259-8
12 Launching New Global Trade Talks:
An Action Agenda   Jeffrey J. Schott, ed.
September 1998   ISBN 0-88132-266-0
13 Japan's Financial Crisis and Its Parallels
to US Experience
Ryoichi Mikitani and Adam S. Posen, eds.
September 2000   ISBN 0-88132-289-X
14 The Ex-Im Bank in the 21st Century:
A New Approach Gary Clyde Hufbauer
and Rita M. Rodriguez, editors
January 2001   ISBN 0-88132-300-4
15 The Korean Diaspora in the World
Economy   C. Fred Bergsten and
Inbom Choi, eds.
January 2003   ISBN 0-88132-358-6
16 Dollar Overvaluation and the World
Economy   C. Fred Bergsten
and John Williamson, eds.
February 2003   ISBN 0-88132-351-9
17 Dollar Adjustment: How Far?
Against What?   C. Fred Bergsten
and John Williamson, eds.
November 2004   ISBN 0-88132-378-0
18 The Euro at Five: Ready for a Global
Role?   Adam S. Posen, editor
April 2005   ISBN 0-88132-380-2
19 Reforming the IMF for the 21st Century
Edwin M. Truman, editor
April 2006   ISBN 0-88132-387-X
                     ISBN 978-0-88132-387-0

WORKS IN PROGRESS

Challenges of Globalization:
Imbalances and Growth
Anders Åslund/Marek Dabrowski, eds.
China's Rise: Challenges and Opportunities
C. Fred Bergsten, Charles Freeman, Nicholas
R. Lardy, and Derek J. Mitchell
US Pension Reform: Lessons from Other
Countries   Martin N. Baily/Jacob Kirkegaard
Reassessing US Trade Policy: Priorities and
Policy Recommendations for the Next Decade
Jeffrey J. Schott
China's Energy Evolution: The Consequences
of Powering Growth at Home and Abroad
Daniel H. Rosen and Trevor Houser
China's Exchange Rates: Options
and Prescriptions
Morris Goldstein and Nicholas R. Lardy
Banking on Basel: The Future of International
Financial Regulation   Daniel K. Tarullo
Global Identity Theft: Economic
and Policy Implications   Catherine L. Mann
Growth and Diversification of International
Reserves   Edwin M. Truman
Financial Regulation after the Subprime
and Credit Crisis   Morris Goldstein
Globalized Venture Capital: Implications
for US Entrepreneurship and Innovation
Catherine L. Mann
Forging a Grand Bargain: Expanding
Trade and Raising Worker Prosperity
Lori Kletzer, J. David Richardson,
and Howard Rosen
East Asian Regionalism and the World
Economy   C. Fred Bergsten
The Strategic Implications of China-Taiwan
Economic Relations   Nicholas R. Lardy
Reform in a Rich Country: Germany
Adam S. Posen
Second among Equals: The Middle-Class
Kingdoms of India and China   Surjit Bhalla
Global Forces, American Faces:
US Economic Globalization at the Grass
Roots   J. David Richardson
Financial Crises and the Future
of Emerging Markets   William R. Cline
Global Services Outsourcing: The Impact
on American Firms and Workers
J. Bradford Jensen, Lori G. Kletzer,
and Catherine L. Mann
Policy Reform in Rich Countries
John Williamson, editor
The Impact of Financial Globalization
William R. Cline
Banking System Fragility
in Emerging Economies
Morris Goldstein and Philip Turner

Australia, New Zealand,
and Papua New Guinea
D. A. Information Services
648 Whitehorse Road
Mitcham, Victoria 3132, Australia
Tel: 61-3-9210-7777
Fax: 61-3-9210-7788
Email: service@dadirect.com.au
www.dadirect.com.au

India, Bangladesh, Nepal, and Sri Lanka
Viva Books Private Limited
Mr. Vinod Vasishtha
4737/23 Ansari Road
Daryaganj, New Delhi 110002
India
Tel: 91-11-4224-2200
Fax: 91-11-4224-2240
Email: viva@vivagroupindia.net
www.vivagroupindia.com

Mexico, Central America, South America,
and Puerto Rico
US PubRep, Inc.
311 Dean Drive
Rockville, MD 20851
Tel: 301-838-9276
Fax: 301-838-9278
Email: c.falk@ieee.org

Asia (*Brunei, Burma, Cambodia, China,*
Hong Kong, Indonesia, Korea, Laos, Malaysia,
Philippines, Singapore, Taiwan, Thailand,
and Vietnam)
East-West Export Books (EWEB)
University of Hawaii Press
2840 Kolowalu Street
Honolulu, Hawaii 96822-1888
Tel: 808-956-8830
Fax: 808-988-6052
Email: eweb@hawaii.edu

Canada
Renouf Bookstore
5369 Canotek Road, Unit 1
Ottawa, Ontario KlJ 9J3, Canada
Tel: 613-745-2665
Fax: 613-745-7660
www.renoufbooks.com

Japan
United Publishers Services Ltd.
1-32-5, Higashi-shinagawa
Shinagawa-ku, Tokyo 140-0002
Japan
Tel: 81-3-5479-7251
Fax: 81-3-5479-7307
Email: purchasing@ups.co.jp
For trade accounts only. Individuals will find
Institute books in leading Tokyo bookstores.

Middle East
MERIC
2 Bahgat Ali Street, El Masry Towers
Tower D, Apt. 24
Zamalek, Cairo
Egypt
Tel. 20-2-7633824
Fax: 20-2-7369355
Email: mahmoud_fouda@mericonline.com
www.mericonline.com

United Kingdom, Europe
(*including Russia and Turkey*), **Africa,**
and Israel
The Eurospan Group
c/o Turpin Distribution
Pegasus Drive
Stratton Business Park
Biggleswade, Bedfordshire
SG18 8TQ
United Kingdom
Tel: 44 (0) 1767-604972
Fax: 44 (0) 1767-601640
Email: eurospan@turpin-distribution.com
www.eurospangroup.com/bookstore

Visit our website at:
www.petersoninstitute.org
E-mail orders to:
petersonmail@presswarehouse.com